THERE'S MORE TO
LIFE
THAN
THE
CORNER OFFICE

THERE'S MORE TO
LIFE
THAN THE
CORNER OFFICE

{ *The Secret to Total Life Prosperity* }

Lamar Smith and Tammy Kling

New York   Chicago   San Francisco
Lisbon   London   Madrid   Mexico City   Milan
New Delhi   San Juan   Seoul   Singapore
Sydney   Toronto

1 2 3 4 5 6 7 8 9 0   DOC/DOC   0 1 0 9

ISBN 978-0-07-160930-2
MHID   0-07-160930-X

McGraw-Hill books are available at special quantity discounts to use as premiums and sales promotions, or for use in corporate training programs. To contact a representative, please visit the Contact Us pages at www.mhprofessional.com.

This book is printed on acid-free paper.

*This effort is dedicated to fellow
travelers who sense that life
will be richer for those who choose
to grow so that they can serve others.
And especially to my wife, Jan,
whose feminine strength inspires me
to find ever more in myself.*

A Crisis of Personal Choice

In a few hundred years, when the history of our time will be written from a long-term perspective, it is likely that the most important event historians will see is not technology, not the Internet, not e-commerce. It is an unprecedented change in the human condition. For the first time—literally—substantial and rapidly growing numbers of people have choices. For the first time, they will have to manage themselves. And society is totally unprepared for it.

—Peter Drucker

INTRODUCTION

In corporate America, there is an office that's coveted above all others. The office in the corner with more windows, a better view, and more privacy is the most desirable, and it is occupied by the highest-ranking executive. The corner office has become symbolic of high performance and success. It's an office that men and women all over the world strive to occupy. It's an office where the fate of others is determined and critical decisions are made that affect whole families, shareholders, and industries. It's an office that I occupied for many years—the office of CEO.

Other worlds have a symbol equivalent to the corner office. No matter the field of endeavor, there is something within it that represents the highest echelon of success, the barometer of achievement, the pot of gold at the end of the rainbow. It's the Gold Medal at the Olympics, the Super Bowl ring in the National Football League, the Champ title in boxing, and the Oscar in the motion picture industry.

The quest begins in the early years, and it is fueled by yearning for the gold star the teacher offers up in the classroom. By the time we're grown, we are so conditioned to achieving and to pursuing the ever-elusive bigger gold star that our lives get out of balance and our true purpose is lost. As the CEO of a large financial firm, my life centered around my PDA and the hectic schedule of managing thousands of people and juggling the various aspects of running a company. From the clients, to the field force, to the employees, regulators, press, and community at large, keeping others happy for long was virtually impossible. Every day was a new turn on the hamster treadmill, and often there was little time to reflect on other aspects of life that really mattered too.

I often reflect on a letter written by a fellow CEO and friend who in the end had lost his health and his family. After retirement, he also burned through his money. To some he had achieved it all, but then he wrote a final letter to his Christmas card list on what would be his final day. He committed suicide. His letter is a masterpiece of justification of decades of poor choices and a totally unbalanced life. My friend's life ended with a lot of things undone. Will yours? Will mine? It depends on our choices. Shall we commit not to die with our music still in us? If so, how do we deliver on that commitment? That question has haunted me for years. This story is a result and is intended to help.

Are you leading your best life with large daily doses of joy and confidence, or do you just exist in the rat race, solely in a quest for achievement? Do you often say "I can't keep doing this" and then fail to make any real changes? A lot of people are simply passengers on the journey of life. They let jobs, events, and relationships enter and exit without much conscious thought or planning about what happens next. This book invites you to leave the passenger seat and become the pilot in command of your own choices.

There's More to Life Than the Corner Office is not about lowering your sights. It is about achieving your own corner office and doing so while maintaining a balanced well-being in five key areas: physical, intellectual, emotional, financial, and spiritual. It is largely a how-to book. It will suggest how to establish a framework to empower your life by identifying your deepest personal values. It will also illustrate how to identify threats to truthful self-appraisal and how to eliminate them. In the end, this book and its easy-to-read story will show the way to a life of purpose, significance, and joy. Is that a tall order? Yes it is, but it is doable and I can show you how, so let's begin.

ONE

I BOARDED THE five o'clock flight to Boston and waited in a long line of travelers herding to the back of the plane. I had missed out on the upgrade to first class, and when I passed through the cabin, I saw the guy who had been just ahead of me on the upgrade list who had taken the last seat. He had a cup of roasted nuts on his tray.

How could this day get any worse?

I found my assigned seat by the lavatory, crammed in at the window. An older man in a crumpled shirt and khakis was sitting in it.

"I'm 27A," I said impatiently, pointing to my boarding pass. I shoved my bag into the overhead bin and waited.

The man smiled. "I'm sorry," he said, sliding out of the row. He stood in the aisle and let me pass. "I'm exhausted. I was hoping to get some sleep on this flight."

I settled into my seat and stared out the window. The man sat down in the more desirable aisle seat. By the time the airplane backed away from the gate and took off, I realized that if I hadn't been in such a rush, I could have just sat down in his seat and traded with him. Figures, I thought. Nothing's gone right today.

The business trip had started with a rude rental car employee. Cars were sold out, and I ended up with a compact instead of the Premium Class I normally rented. I had an argument with the woman at the counter even though I had flashed my Gold rental car card. Nothing worked. When I arrived at my meeting, the CEO wasn't there. The lightweight associate who substituted for him was an idiot and wouldn't even sign my nondisclosure agreement because he couldn't see the accretion, the magic of investment banking. So instead of enjoying the planned celebration dinner with new clients at Jardinière, I was headed home early—empty-handed and not sure what I was going to tell my boss, John Carter. All of it had been a colossal waste of time.

A flight attendant stopped in the aisle. She had long auburn hair that fell to her shoulders. "Can I get you anything?" she asked.

I glanced at the gold name badge on her vest. "Yes, Brittany," I said. "I'd like a vodka tonic. One lime."

"Sure thing." The old man was asleep now, and she leaned over him and placed a napkin on my tray.

In minutes she was back with the tonic, a little bottle of vodka, and a bag of pretzels. I noticed a gold cross dangled from her neck. "Anything else?"

Cracking the seal on the vodka, "I'm fine, now."

"That's a beautiful suit you're wearing," she said.

"Thank you. It's an Oxford custom."

"Really? I knew it was something expensive. Are you traveling on business?"

"Yes. I'm an investment banker. I've got over a million miles on this airline."

The man in the aisle seat opened his eyes and asked for a Coke.

"Certainly," she said.

I took a sip of vodka, felt it stinging my throat. "Brittany, could I ask for one more thing?" I pulled a business card from my suit jacket and handed it to her. She studied the gold letters engraved on the front. Investment banker. "Give me a call sometime," I said. "I'll take you to dinner."

She tucked the card into her pocket and smiled. When she walked away, the man in my row chuckled.

"What's so funny?"

"She had a big diamond on her left hand," he said, grinning.

"I'm aware of that."

"You noticed? And you still asked her out?"

"Princess cut, with two baguettes."

"You rolled the dice anyway. Gotta hand you that much."

"That only makes it more interesting."

He took a sip of his Coke. "Okay, I see. You like the chase."

"Isn't that a big part of life? The chase?"

The man smiled, settled back in his seat. "I used to think that way."

I bet it was a long time ago, I thought.

I pulled out my laptop and reviewed the notes from the meeting. Maybe I could resurrect the thing next month. Give the client some time, and then make another visit but this time loaded with the big guns. I'd e-mail the nondisclosure again when I got back to the office and give the client more information about the value we are proposing. All I need to do is get past the gatekeepers, to the real decision maker.

"Are you headed to home, or away from home?" asked aisle guy.

"I live in Boston," I replied.

"What part?"

I downed the last of the vodka, straight from the miniature bottle. His small talk was beginning to annoy me. "Cambridge, near MIT. You?"

"I live in a little town called Marblehead," he said.

"Were you on business? I assume you were by the way you're dressed."

Wow, this old guy was a rocket scientist. What was it that tipped you off? I wanted to say.

"I'm an investment banker. I was in San Francisco for a meeting with the CEO of Legacy Technology Corporation, but at the last minute he decided not to sit in. He sent in an empty suit instead. Now I get to ride in the back of the bus because I have an assistant who can't get the upgrade thing right." I wished for another vodka tonic. "These seats are murder on your back."

"I understand," he said, extending his hand. "I'm Al."

I shook it quickly. "Patrick Mitchell."

"So you're in banking. Why did you decide on that particular field?"

I paused, then stared out the window. "To do a lot of deals and make a lot of money. Isn't that why we all do what we do?"

I ordered another drink from the next flight attendant who passed by; she came back with two bottles of vodka for the price of one.

"No, not really," the man replied.

"Excuse me?"

"I don't think most people work just to make a lot of money. I believe there are other considerations that drive people, particularly as time goes by."

You've gotta be kidding me. Is he for real?

"C'mon, unless you work for a nonprofit or are some sort of activist, that's why people work. To make money. It's how the game of life is played."

"Intriguing," he said.

"You don't agree?"

"Well, I didn't say that. But tell me this, what's the purpose of all the money you make? What will you do with it?"

I decided to change the subject. His questions were wearing me out. "So I suppose you're retired?"

"No," he laughed. "Not exactly."

I looked out the window where the clouds were swirling in a mysterious shade of pink. I leaned back, closed my eyes. This guy was old and clearly not a player in my world.

I realized I had been dozing when the pilot made an announcement. We'd be landing in 30 minutes. I thought back to the times Hannah, my soon-to-be ex-wife, would insist on meeting me at Logan. No matter how late the flight arrived, she was always there, waiting at the curb. One cold night she even showed up in her bathrobe and slippers, half-asleep behind the wheel. When I looked back across the row, aisle guy was sleeping. I tugged on his sleeve. He opened his eyes and focused slowly as if he'd forgotten where he was.

"I need to go to the bathroom," I said.

He stood and let me pass by. When I got back, he was still standing in the aisle. "You have a business card?" he asked.

"I'm not sure I have any left," I said, patting my pockets. I remembered what a consultant had once told our team. Business cards are gold. Share them wisely. I didn't like to hand them out to just anyone. After a while I gave up and pulled a card from the breast pocket of my suit. The older flight attendant stopped at our aisle, touching aisle guy's elbow. "That was so considerate of you to give up your first class seat for that soldier," she said.

"No problem," he told her. "It's going to be a long road ahead for him."

I listened to their conversation but couldn't believe what I was hearing. This guy is insane, I thought. He had a first class seat on a six-hour red-eye and he gave it up?

I closed my eyes and tried to sleep, but before I knew it, we were on the ground, unloading. I grabbed my briefcase and headed to the front of the plane, and when I passed through the first class cabin, I saw a man in a military uniform still sitting there, waiting. Most of one leg was missing, the pant leg tucked under. At the jet bridge, a porter with a wheelchair waited.

Outside at the curb, I spotted aisle guy again, this time standing with a limousine driver beside a black Lincoln.

I did a double take. The driver wore a dark suit, and he hoisted the man's bag into the trunk of the car. Al walked back inside the airport, and I approached the limo and looked at the driver, then the car. "You picking up Al?"

"Yes," he said. "You know Mr. Crafton? I'm his personal driver."

"Mr. Crafton, uh, yes," I lied. I didn't really know him, but something about the name seemed familiar. I rolled it over in my mind.

"Al Crafton! You've got to be kidding me. That's Al Crafton, the chairman of Castle Investment Corporation? The Al Crafton on the cover of *Business Life* magazine?"

"Yes. You implied you knew him."

My hand shook, and I switched my briefcase from one fist to the other. "I sat next to him on the plane, and we talked, but I didn't really place him. He seemed so, so . . ."

"So normal?"

"Well, his clothes were wrinkled and everything, and I just assumed . . ."

"He was traveling on personal business," the driver said. "He was helping the son of a friend of his who is now deceased. The son is having some problems, and I believe Al was with the family all day and had no time to change." The driver smiled. "He had to get back for an important board meeting tomorrow."

I nodded, dumbfounded at my stupidity. Why hadn't I gotten his business card?

"I've worked for him for 10 years," the driver said proudly.

I stood there, stunned. The man on the plane seemed like every other old man. The executives and important people sat in first class. That was where deals were made, why guys like me tried to get upgrades. Literally millions of dollars of business deals had their seeds planted over scotch in first class on flights crisscrossing the country. I looked back toward the glass windows in the terminal and tried to recall every word we'd spoken, and I realized I couldn't have screwed it up more.

"Some things are not as they seem," the driver said.

TWO

THE 10 DAYS since San Francisco had been a blur. The one exception to the hectic demands at work had been a phone conversation with Hannah. We talked about everything but the legalities, though the divorce lurked in the darkness.

"We should talk about the papers," I said finally.

"There's no rush," she replied. "Is there?"

I slept better that night than I had in weeks.

I strolled into the office the next day to find 152 e-mails in my inbox. The calls began rolling in the minute I hit the door. It wasn't until noon that I had a lull. My assistant Stacy was just outside my door in her cubicle handling a stream of endless calls, e-mails, and, at one point, an angry client.

"He wants to talk to you," she said.

"I'm not here."

"But . . ."

"Didn't you understand? I am not here. Can't you see I've got a million things going today?"

There were client calls to return, two deals to resurrect, and an analysis due tomorrow. I was top guy in my department, and it was because I had nothing tying me down. No kids, no wife, not even a cat. There were four bankers in my group, and two were married. The third was a divorced woman with kids who kept her out of the office more than she was in. I looked at the little reminder sign above my desk.

The first runner-up is the top loser.

"Isn't that the truth!" I said out loud.

Stacy appeared in the doorway. "The luncheon at the Harbor Club is today," she said. "Just a reminder."

"Got it," I said, waving her off.

The Harbor Club was an elite location. Leaders from Boston's top firms would hear from a Washington insider about the priorities of the upcoming session of Congress. There would be several of my firm's most influential executives gathered in the most exclusive location in the city. You had to be a member to get in or be invited by one, and my firm had a business membership for the executive committee. I'd been invited by John Carter, my boss and also a rising star at the firm, to sit in on the luncheon and learn. I think he intended it to be a pat on the back.

The night after my return flight from San Francisco, I hadn't slept more than a few hours. I drove home from the airport, opened my laptop, and poured myself a stiff drink. As I sat in the comfort of my home office, I Googled Al Crafton and tried to think about creative ways to contact him.

I even considered sending an e-mail, but I could not find his address. I text messaged Stacy before the sun came up and asked her to arrange a meeting and to research Crafton to find everything she could about the deals he was involved in. Crafton's company was valued at a market cap of $5 billion, and it had a run rate of over $4 billion in annual revenues. Castle Investments had sustained a high, double-digit growth rate for over a decade by balancing organic growth and some well-planned acquisitions. Crafton's nickname on Wall Street was "Al Craftsman" because of his skill.

Al Crafton had been featured in a recent article in a business magazine as one of America's 50 most influential businesspeople, mainly for his role in executing a series of strategic mergers in the financial services industry. Some had even credited him with helping politicians draw up and pass the law that made it possible for banking, investment, and insurance services to be offered by one firm, which changed the industry! He was a trailblazer, for sure.

Crafton was a respected business leader, admired for his entrepreneurial finesse, and he also headed up some nonprofit thing to help starving people or something. Another article said that he had first entered business when he was still in high school, selling books door to door.

———

Stacy appeared at my desk, chewing the end of a pencil. "Excuse me, sir. But your car service is downstairs, ready to take you to the Harbor Club."

"That's lead paint, you're chewing on."

She slid the pencil behind her ear. "And Mr. Carter has been asking for your weekly activity report."

"When's the deadline?"

"Five o'clock. Yesterday."

"I'll get it done. I'll be with him today at the lunch at the Harbor Club."

"You know how he is. As soon as he gets back to the office, he'll be reviewing those reports, first thing."

"Okay," I grumbled.

"Is there anything else you need me to do?" she asked.

"Yes. Call Al Crafton's office when I'm gone and try

to arrange a brief meeting. Carter would be blown away if he knew I was meeting with Crafton. He'd forget all about the report."

"I already called twice, sir. I didn't get past the receptionist."

"Call three times."

I watched as she left my office. Stacy was pretty and professional, but personalitywise, she was about as vanilla as they come with just a little edge. Mainly, she put up with me. I hadn't put the moves on her, and I didn't really know why. I'd been distracted by a blonde I had met on a business flight several months ago, and most of the weekends were taken up that way.

———

John Carter had been the head of our department for three years. He was a tough executive vice president in his midforties with two kids, a wife, and a reputation for firing people from time to time just for grins. But Carter and I got along just fine. We were good for each other. I was his star and I was learning from him. He had a flair for making deal negotiations seem easy, and he could have a client seeing his point of view within minutes. But when you crossed him or didn't do your job right, watch out. I actually saw him fire a high-performing employee for showing up 15 minutes late for a client dinner. The guy had been at his kids' soccer match and got hung up in traffic, but Carter didn't care.

I had been on the blunt end of his rage only once when I had to listen to 10 solid minutes of digital-quality swearing on my voice mail. If I could arrange a meeting with Al Crafton, I'd move up the food chain a link or two.

I grabbed my suit jacket and flew down the hall to the elevator. The ride to the Harbor Club was 10 minutes, and I spent the entire time on my BlackBerry answering e-mails. When I stepped out of the car, I lingered at the curb in awe of the club. The building was covered in glass, like a tower of mirrors. You could see reflections from every angle.

I stepped inside the building and took the elevator to the penthouse level. Inside the lobby of the club the walls were trimmed in dark burgundy fabric. Gold-framed paintings of Old English scenes with hunting dogs lined the reception area, and further down the hall, small groups of older men in expensive suits gathered in private rooms. I saw Carter standing outside a room with our firm's name on a framed card by the door.

"Morning, Patrick," he said nodding.

"Good morning, John."

Some associates called him "Sir," but I avoided using that word most of the time. I didn't see much difference between the two of us and wanted him to know it.

I shook hands with the other men he was standing with, recognizing them as senior executives. I was by far the youngest. Someone tapped my shoulder.

"Hello, Patrick. We meet again."

I turned abruptly to see Al Crafton standing before me, grinning.

He wore a dark suit, and a shirt with onyx cufflinks. "Fancy meeting you here," he said. He reached for my hand and shook it firmly. Before I knew it, he and Carter were introducing themselves to each other and shaking hands too.

Crafton slid a business card into my palm. "Are you available to have breakfast next Tuesday?" he asked.

I looked down at the card, stunned. I opened my mouth, but the words wouldn't come.

"What are you doing here?" I said awkwardly. It came out all wrong.

"Nothing's an accident, my friend. You should know that by now."

"Of course he's available for breakfast," Carter interrupted.

"Yes, I am. Of course. Where?"

Crafton turned to Carter. "You've got an impressive young man working for you," he said. "See you Tuesday, Patrick. Details on the back of the card."

Crafton walked away. When he was gone, the others huddled around me like flies.

"You know Al Crafton?" asked Carter.

"Where did you meet him?" asked another.

Carter took charge and steered me away to a corner, where we could talk alone.

"This could be huge for our company and for both of us if you can gain traction with Al Crafton. Many have tried and all have failed. He's never done business with the firm." I nodded, feeling Crafton's card gaining weight in my palm.

"Listen, Patrick," Carter started, his eyes boring into mine. "Before you joined Goodwin and Meyer, for a period of about two years, two of our best partners worked closely under the direction of the Boston managing director herself, Patricia Redmond, trying to get Crafton's business. It actually got embarrassing because our three best talents were never able to even get into Crafton's corner office. They must have tried six or eight different approaches and tactics. Nothing. Finally Redmond just called Crafton and asked why he wouldn't give us the time of day. Crafton said our two cultures were not compatible, whatever the hell that means."

"Wow."

"Do you get what I am telling you here?"

My mind was spinning. Why would Crafton invite me to breakfast after I completely misread him on the airplane?

"Yes, I get it. Make the most of this opportunity."

"No, it's much stronger than that. Sell your soul, commit a crime if you must, but keep the dialogue with Crafton open. Do whatever it takes, anything and everything! Now do you get it?"

"Got it."

"You have no other assignments until further notice. Focus on Crafton and Castle Investments alone. Learn all you can and think about it all the time. Find a way to get in there! And you are to personally and immediately brief me day or night of every single development. Are we clear?"

"Crystal." Carter asked me to repeat the instructions he had just given me. Every line.

When he walked away, I stared at the business card in disbelief. Al Crafton had scrawled a meeting place on the back.

Tuesday 8 a.m.
Fred's Diner
Quincy Street

THREE

Sᴇʟʟ ʏᴏᴜʀ sᴏᴜʟ. Commit a crime if you must . . .

———

I made the turn onto Massachusetts Avenue and thought about what Crafton had said. Nothing's an accident. I couldn't believe my luck, and I had been awake most of Monday night thinking about the meeting and what I'd say.

I had taken the BMW to the car wash, and I had the inside supercleaned just in case. Attention to detail; the mark of a superstar. I wore my finest suit and made sure I chose a shirt with heavy starch and cufflinks. Crafton would have a limited amount of time. I'd study his words carefully, figure him out, and wait for the right moment to tell him what he wanted to hear.

I glanced over at the file on the passenger seat. Stacy had spent hours compiling information on Crafton's company, and then she printed it all and brought it in to me Monday morning, along with a printed map to the diner.

I drove and studied the map, and though the neighborhood seemed like it was getting shaky, the map was clear. I turned onto Quincy Street, and four blocks later, a sign for Fred's Sunshine Diner hung above a doorway in an unimpressive brick building. No way! I found a spot on the street and parked. I dialed Stacy's cell phone.

"Hello?"

"Please tell me you didn't give me the wrong directions!"

"What??"

"What the hell is wrong with you? This is a dive. It has to be the wrong Fred's café."

"Diner," she said.

"Whatever. This one has plywood on some of the windows. This isn't a place Al Crafton would select for a meeting. I need a jumpsuit with 'Hank' stitched on the front to fit in here."

"But I took the address from the business card you gave me," she explained.

A Land Rover pulled in and parked two spaces in front of me, and a man in a plaid flannel work shirt and jeans jumped out and headed for the door. It looked like Al Crafton. I could not believe my eyes.

"I have to go. Never mind. He's here."

I leapt out of the BMW and followed him inside, catching him just as he arrived at a booth.

"Patrick! You found it." He grabbed my hand and shook it firmly. "And you are right on time."

A waitress handed him a steaming cup of coffee in a heavy mug. She wore an apron littered with various pins with sayings on them. A yellow smiley face pin on her pocket had a frown, instead of a smile.

"Thanks, Marge," Crafton said. "You're looking nice today."

"Oh, you old sweetie." She looked my way. "Coffee for you, son?"

"Yes, black."

I looked around at the place. It was packed. I was the only one in the diner wearing a tie. "So you come here much?" I asked.

"Every Tuesday," Crafton said. "I take the day off on Tuesdays and work nearby." He looked around and exchanged smiles and a wave with a man two booths over. "And Saturday mornings too, usually with my wife."

"You drive all the way out here on a Saturday? Doesn't that hurt your golf game?"

"Sure!" He laughed. "But I was never much into golf anyway."

The waitress came back and slid the coffee and a menu in front of me and continued to another table without breaking stride.

"This probably isn't the kind of place you normally frequent, is it? You like the Harbor Club, I suppose."

I nodded. "Yes."

"That place is a bit stuffy for me, personally," Crafton said. "But I just show up where they tell me to."

I was dying to know who "they" were, but the waitress came back for my order.

"I'll have the Tuesday breakfast special. Eggs over easy, with wheat toast."

She nodded and left. Crafton didn't order.

"So you're not married?" Crafton asked.

"Nope. Well, technically, yes. We've been legally separated almost a year now. How about you?"

Crafton nodded. "Next month will be 38 years!"

"Don't get me wrong," I said, hoping not to sound casual about a failed marriage. "My wife is wonderful. Everything was great when we first met. But she never liked me working so much. I told her we'd start a family after I made EVP. I guess she got impatient."

Crafton contemplated me for a moment. "Any regrets?"

"Regret is for losers. So no, I don't have any regrets. I miss her, sure, but I can't look at what might have been. Life's not a country western song."

"Do you think you'll eventually have a wife and family?"

I shifted uncomfortably in my seat. I needed to stay focused on winning his business, but Hannah's face popped into my head. She was laughing, wearing that white gauzy dress from the time we vacationed in Cabo, on the beach. Where did that flashback come from? Remember the game plan, I told myself. Listen, dissect, feed him back what he wants to hear.

"I haven't given it much thought, actually. I don't want to lose my edge, I know that much."

"Lose your edge? What's that mean, exactly?"

The waitress returned and gave us both a refill.

"You know, get married, have kids, gain weight, get a little comfortable. Most people stop thinking about their original commitment to success. They get older, get married, and slow down. When you take your eye off the ball, you get less competitive. Not going to happen to me!"

Crafton smiled. "I see. Do you think that's what has happened to me?"

"Let's face it, most people aren't you. Obviously that's not what happened to you, and that's why I'm being so candid. I know you can relate to what I'm saying. Most get older and lose their edge for their career. They get too comfortable. But you didn't, and I won't either." My eyes settled on the hands wrapped around his coffee mug. They were large, with deep crevices. More like a working man's hands than a CEO's. Most executives I knew had manicured fingernails. "You're like the Tiger Woods of the business world," I finished.

Crafton said nothing.

"I saw an interview with Tiger recently," I continued. "And he said he doesn't play to come in second. He plays to win."

"How old are you?" Crafton asked.

"Almost 30."

"I see. I am 64. That puts us 35 years apart. I believe you and I are a lot alike except for those years and the many chances they have given me to twist my ankles on the uneven pavement of life."

"Really?"

"Yes. And based on the years between us, I'd say there's nothing wrong with having a competitive spirit, but even Tiger doesn't win every time. He's a world-class athlete, and winning is part of the sport of competition. But in the real world, where we all work together, it's about leveraging the strengths of each other to win. Life and the business world are much more like team sports than golf."

I pretended to sip my coffee.

"But the sports analogy falls short if you think others have to lose for you to win in business. The best strategy is for everyone to win. It's a matter of respect."

The waitress showed up with two plates and slid them in front of us. I folded the napkin over my tie and shirt, and took a bite of eggs.

"Are they good?" Crafton asked, digging into his breakfast.

"Better than I expected. I usually eat breakfast on the run if at all."

I glanced at my watch. I was beginning to feel like we were wasting too much time. I needed to get him back on track.

"Can I change the subject?" I asked. "I have something I really want to know."

"Sure, Patrick, anything. Especially if you weren't comfortable with where we were going, about respect and teamwork."

"No, it's not that . . . I hear you. But I'm an only child," I said. "I'm an individualist. Maybe I don't know what it's like to be on a team."

"Just be sure you don't cop out," Crafton said.

"So you said you worked nearby every Tuesday. Do you have a big project going on down here in this area?"

Crafton shook his head. "Nope."

"Then why do you come down here? It doesn't seem like a powerful economic region, to say the least."

"Because I like to. And because I can. One of the most important things I do is spend time down here on Tuesdays. You'll see why."

I drank a sip of the water from the hard plastic glass in front of me. It tasted faintly like chlorine.

"Can I ask you another question?"

"Sure, Patrick."

"What did you mean when you said 'there are no accidents,' and why did you ask me to have breakfast with you?"

"Which question do you want me to answer first?" Crafton said. "Both questions are intertwined. I asked you to breakfast because I don't believe in accidents."

I stared at him, waiting for the rest of it.

"And my many years of experience tell me that we could teach each other a few things. I'm at a stage of life when I want to multiply what I have learned, especially the things I learned the hard way. I want to share with others. I'm in the investment business, but not just financial investments anymore. I really enjoy investing time with other people now."

I was more confused than ever, but I nodded as if I knew exactly what he was talking about.

"Let me ask you the same question," he said. "What do you hope to get from meeting with me? Can you be courageously honest? Will you say it out loud?"

I felt heat rising to my face. He was testing me.

"To state the obvious, Mr. Crafton, I'm an investment banker and you're the CEO of a firm that's very active and successful in mergers and acquisitions. I want your business." I was warming up. "What will it take to get it?"

His eyes lit up. He seemed pleased. "Now we are getting somewhere," he said. "I like your honesty. Continue it, okay? Reflecting back, what did you think of me on the flight from San Francisco when we first met? No BS allowed, by the way."

"What do you mean? I don't understand the question."

"It's simple. What did you think of me when we first met?"

"I had no idea who you were. I probably should have recognized you, but I didn't. You were dressed casually. Your pants were wrinkled. You didn't look like a CEO."

Crafton said nothing, so I worked to fill the silence.

"I was tired and at the end of a disappointing day. I was frustrated by many things, including having to sit in coach, blocked into a window seat."

Crafton reached into his pocket and pulled out some loose bills, then placed a twenty on the table. "So let me summarize," he said. "You were focused on you, I was a nuisance to you, and apparently I could not offer you anything of value, so you discounted me as a nonperson. You even paused and considered not handing me a business card when I politely asked for one. That about right?"

I lowered my head, busted. This was not going well. I saw my chances for hero status at my firm circling the drain.

"Yes, that's exactly the way it was," I admitted.

Crafton sat back in the booth, eyeing me.

"I'm sorry," I tried.

"Tell me, when did you figure out you had missed an opportunity?"

"I spoke to your driver briefly at Logan and then, later, put two and two together."

"Ah, Anthony. He has been with me for years. He's pretty talkative."

"I learned all I could about you and had my assistant try to reach your staff to set up a brief visit. She didn't have much luck. Then I ran into you, or more accurately, you ran into me at the Harbor Club."

"Is there anything else?"

"Nope," I shrugged. "Should there be?"

"Well, Patrick, can I talk with you for a moment about something I refer to as 'evaluated experience'?"

I nodded. I was eager to learn anything I could about his philosophy. The more I learned, the more information I had that I could report to Carter.

"Each significant experience contains a lesson or two—that is, if we care to harvest them. We have to learn to be bold, honest, and analytical to dig out those lessons that can make us better."

I was wondering where he was going, and I guess it showed on my face.

"Experience without evaluation is simply exposure. No gain results. The gain comes from learning by evaluating. You want a real-life example?"

"That would help."

"When we first met, everybody you had dealt with had let you down somehow. They just did not 'get it.' The rental car employees, your secretary, the businessmen you had met that day, and even me. We were all a disappointment to you in some way, and it was no secret that you felt that way. True feelings usually come across, you know."

I said nothing.

"Continue with your honesty, Patrick, and answer this for me. I observed that almost no one you had dealt with that day was worthy of you. Fair statement?"

I did not want his business this much. Why was he analyzing me this way?

"Patrick, the most successful people are the ones who ask themselves the hard questions and confront the truth even if it isn't pretty. I am not judging you. I am sharing a deep insight that took me years to figure out, so here it is: Each and every person is incalculably valuable. Each person we meet is as valuable and deserving of our respect as every other. No one is 'less.' You and I are not 'more.' Even someone who is deeply challenged financially or someone who is limited physically or mentally will have compensating gifts and abilities. Discount no one."

He stopped, looked down at his coffee. I waited, but that was it.

"So you think I fundamentally discount others?"

"I didn't say that. But maybe you should think about it. As you do, contemplate the issue of integrity as it relates."

"Integrity?"

"Yes, a simple definition is being the same on the outside as on the inside. No pretense, but the same through and through."

"Okay, I'll think about it, but, Mr. Crafton, can I take us back to a question I asked earlier?"

"Sure, bet I can guess which one. How can you get my business, right?"

"Does that offend you? The fact that I'm interested in your business?"

"Not at all. Remember, you remind me of my younger self. Just be real with me, Patrick. I like to know people before I do business with them. At some point I'll give you and your firm a shot at convincing me that we might benefit one another, and actually, you are Goodwin and Meyer's best hope of changing my view of them. But right now that's a steep hill to climb."

I had no real clue what was on his mind, but I didn't want any more of his wisdom for now. I stared at him. I wondered if I had lost control.

"You're like Dr. Phil," I said, trying to make things light. "His delivery is kind of harsh, but if you can handle it, the lessons are there."

Despite all my game planning and preparation for whatever might come up at breakfast, I had been totally unprepared for this.

"On the airplane you were clear you want to make lots of money," he said. "I asked what you would do with it. You changed the subject and never replied. Will you tell me now?"

I wondered if this was a trick question. Money is its own reward.

"Security, the good life, respect from others mostly. Money is the scoreboard. Making and having money is the way people win, and I want to be a winner."

"I see."

"Is that the answer you were looking for?"

"It's not about me, Patrick. There is no one correct answer. I simply suggest money is a means to an end, not an end to itself. Money can power you to act more consistently with your values. Wait until the coming weeks, when we get into the hard but productive values."

"The coming weeks?"

"Yes, Patrick, I propose we meet for breakfast and talk weekly when we can for the next few weeks. Either one of us can end it whenever he wants to. Are you game?"

Well, Carter may not kill me after all, I thought. I still have a chance.

I pushed forward in my seat. "Meetings with Al Crafton? Are you kidding me? Of course I want to meet next week."

"But I do have two points of order. First, let's get on a first-name basis. I am Al, and second, I suggest we choose topics to talk about in advance. For instance, for next week's meeting, I want you to think on the principle of evaluated experience. That's the example I gave you from my observation of you when we first met."

"Okay," I said, nodding.

"You want to jot all this on a napkin?"

I pulled out my BlackBerry and opened the memo icon. "I'll take notes here," I said. "I've got a Crafton file now."

He smiled. "Study the term and process of 'target fixation.' You can find it on the Internet. And think about the power of planning. Think about the process of planning and what it offers you."

I took notes. "Three things. Evaluated experience, the power of planning, and target fixation. Same time and place?"

"Yes." Crafton smiled. He gave me his cell number, and I punched it into my BlackBerry as fast as he said the numbers, hardly believing it. He paid the check and left a hefty tip. "You have time to follow me around the corner? I have something to show you."

I followed Crafton around the block, to a building with a sign that said HOPE Center above the door. Crafton explained that it was a neighborhood center for those out of work, displaced, homeless, or just "lost" to come and get help. The first thing that would happen for new clients was an evaluation of their immediate needs and they would be offered expeditious help on the basis of those needs. For instance, if people had no money, they would be put to work, at least part-time, doing simple tasks to give them a chance to earn a little cash, stabilize, and begin to restore their dignity.

We walked in and Crafton found a disheveled young man sitting on a stool by the door. He wore black jeans and sneakers. "How you doing today, Stan?"

The man smiled and gave Crafton a big hug. "All right," he said.

Crafton moved through the building shaking hands, and I followed like a lost puppy. He ducked into a small office for about five minutes where he talked with an administrator about the program, while I waited in the doorway. When it was over, he explained the new building campaign and how his firm's foundation was helping to fund it with a matching program.

"HOPE Center does not deal in charity," he said. "It's all about empowering people and giving them opportunity. It's about the restoration of dignity."

"Are these people who have committed crimes?"

"Some," he said. "But not in all cases. Sometimes they've just had hard luck, or poor role models to follow. Either way, the ultimate goal is to enable the clients to be fully productive members of society pulling their own weight."

I thought about his choice of words. Clients.

I drove toward the office, on cloud nine. I knew Carter was anxious to hear about it, and I had to figure out what to tell him, so I pulled over and thought about it, making notes. I decided to describe most of our time as chitchat, quoting Crafton that he wanted to get to know me before "putting me and my firm on the team."

I would also proudly report the series of weekly meetings and the personal cell phone number. My stock was on the rise. I drove a little faster after I had my report figured out. I wanted to deliver this one personally, not on voice mail.

There are no accidents.

FOUR

THE FOLLOWING TUESDAY I drove to Fred's and parked right out front again. I wore jeans and a light blue t-shirt, my suit hanging in the BMW for after breakfast.

I had spent much more time preparing for this break-fast meeting, and I had something to say on each of the topics Crafton had assigned. During the week I had collected more and more questions and thoughts, my mind reeling like a tornado. What kind of work was he involved in each day? I knew all about his company, but what projects filled the calendar of a world-renowned CEO? Most of all, I wondered, who is this guy, and what does he want with me? For the entire week John Carter had been a thorn in my side, interrogating me about my progress with Crafton. The interruptions were distracting. Carter wanted an audience with Crafton in the worst way.

This week, I made a point to arrive at the diner 30 minutes early. I was calm, and in control. I chose the booth right next to the one from last week, with Marge serving. I ordered coffee and was on the second cup when Crafton walked in.

I glanced at the three-by-five card in front of me on the table. I had written the topics Crafton had mentioned in our last meeting down the middle:

- *Evaluated experience*
- *Power of planning*
- *Target fixation*

The last one was easy. I had found tons of information on the Internet about it. "Target fixation" is the condition of becoming so singularly focused on a particular goal or objective that one ignores other important factors, even to the point of one's own detriment. While there were other examples given, it seemed the term has its roots in attack pilots' becoming so focused on the ground targets they were bombing or strafing that they would actually forget to pull off of the target in time and plow into the ground. Clearly that qualified as too much of a good thing, but I had admiration for people who were aggressive in business. Most people were lazy. How could target fixation in my world be bad?

Crafton walked over. Marge showed up with coffee right away, just the way he liked it. I rose to greet him and awkwardly bumped my hip on the edge of the table, splashing coffee.

"Oh, sorry."

"No problem, we'll clean it up. How are you, Patrick?" We shook hands.

"I've been looking forward to meeting again," I said.

Crafton glanced at the three-by-five card. "I see you have some notes. Does that mean you remembered the assignment?"

I nodded my head. "Absolutely."

"Did I take time away from your job? I certainly hope not."

"Right now you are my job," I said laughing. I wanted to take the comment back as soon as I saw his expression.

"Oh, I see. So they've put the pit bull on me in full force, have they?"

"Well, the docket has been cleared, for sure. I suppose I'm to have target fixation on Al Crafton right now."

We both laughed, and Marge swept by with a cloth. She brought us both more coffee and took our orders. "Same thing as last time?" she asked. We both nodded.

Crafton looked at the three-by-five. "Okay, tell me

whatcha got." He listened intently as I explained the term I had researched on Wikipedia.

"So do you think target fixation is a good thing overall?" he asked.

I paused and thought about how he'd want me to answer the question. "Well, insufficient focus on goals is rampant in corporate America. No one is focused. Everyone is lazy. I think my target fixation, if that's what you want to call it, gives me a huge advantage."

"Read your definition again," he said.

"'Target fixation' is such intense focus on a particular objective that you ignore other important factors even to the point of your own detriment."

I put the card on the table. "See, target fixation is good in some circumstances and bad in others. Actually now that I think about it, I guess 'target focus' would be a good thing and 'target fixation,' the step beyond focus, that's where the problems arise."

Al seemed pleased. "And why would you want to focus on a target?"

"You focus on something because you want to see it clearly."

"So would you accept the term 'target clarity' as a good thing and 'target fixation' as the extension to be avoided?"

I shrugged. "When you put it that way, it seems obvious. It's just a word game."

"But it can be overdone, right?"

"I guess," I said weakly. I really didn't see how it could be overdone. "If you're a fighter pilot, I suppose."

"The target is the key, Patrick. It's good to have goals, and to have your sights set firmly. The fixation occurs when everything else is ignored."

I looked at him and said nothing.

"Like your marriage," he said.

"Ouch."

Crafton laughed. "What was that line Jack Nicholson made famous?"

"You can't handle the truth!" We both said.

In some ways, Crafton was right. The truth is often hard to swallow.

"See, the attack pilot in the mode of delivering the attack must maintain some awareness of the factors that can destroy him," Crafton said. "Those include his fuel state, how his engine is running, the defenses being put up by the enemy, and even his position within his own formation so as to avoid a collision. When the attack pilot rolls in for the attack pass, he has to be critically aware of altitude, airspeed, and his angle of dive. Failure to pay attention to any of these factors, which might get out of kilter, can result in the loss of life and therefore the loss of ability to sustain long-term performance."

"How do you know all of that?"

Crafton ignored the question. "In other words, over-focusing on just the target can result in everything going down the drain. The same is true in life. To sustain excellent business performance, you must pay attention to areas of life that have the ability to drag you down completely. Business executives who fixate on their careers will often find that they achieve all that they once desired in career success, but they may wind up without any money at all! That's because even though they made it, they lost it because they failed to operate within the principles that govern wealth building."

I nodded. His words resonated. "Like my dad. He made a lot of money, but he died of a heart attack when I was 15. He left us nothing but debt."

"I'm sorry, Patrick. A lot of men do the same thing. They work themselves to death with nothing to show for it. Others work their way up the ladder and sacrifice their health or their relationship with their wife and children in the process."

We sat for a while in silence. I tasted my eggs and took a bite of the hot-buttered toast.

"Al, why are you spending so much time on this subject? You must think I am messing this up, right?" I looked him straight in the eye, doing my best to hold my ground.

"Patrick, that's not for me to say. I just thought it was

worth pointing out the principle so that you could evaluate your own experience."

My BlackBerry buzzed. I checked it, and it was a text from Stacy to call when I could.

"But you think I've screwed up my deal with Hannah, don't you?"

"First off, it's not a deal, Patrick. It was a vow. And I didn't say you screwed it up." He sat back against the wall in the booth. "But I do know it's worth pointing out the principle so that you can have the benefit of self-evaluation."

"I know. I need to rethink my life. I've been thinking a lot about that lately. In fact, I've been so focused on my career that I am now separated from my wife."

"Have you given much consideration to the process of evaluating your experiences thoughtfully?"

"Give me an example of what you mean. Where are you going with this?"

"Evaluated experiences. That was another one of the topics assigned, remember? Have you reconsidered how you came across to me on the flight from San Francisco?"

"Yes, I regret that I seemed so self-focused and judgmental in that situation."

Al leaned forward and eased his mug to the side. "Patrick, this is a very important question. Are you paying attention?"

"I am."

"And will you be thoughtful and honest?"

"Yes, absolutely."

"Are you more sorry that you came across to me as self-focused and judgmental, or is your deeper regret that you actually are self-focused and judgmental?"

I remembered that Al had said integrity is being the same on the inside as on the outside, through and through. That's what he was getting at.

"Honestly, I'm not sure," I admitted. "Maybe I regret both. I regret that I actually felt that way, and I regret that I showed that side of me. It just comes naturally."

"Patrick, you're showing some real promise here. I like your guts. One thing I've learned in my lifetime is that humans have a great capacity to produce and grow, yet most only scratch the surface. Growth is an offshoot of proper planning. Tell me what you see as the benefits of planning."

I thought about it for a moment. Had I really been a good planner? Most things seemed to just come my way. "I guess if I think about it, planning is important to help set a specific goal. In business it's also important to plan to get the team thinking the same thing, to identify resources, know-how, processes needed, and to lay out a timeline. Planning would also be important to establish milestones to measure progress."

Al nodded. "Good. All true, but you missed one and it's the one I want to drive toward. It relates to the milestones idea. If you plan, you establish a course, right?"

"Yes, that works, and some of the waypoints on the course to completion are the milestones."

"Agreed, so my point is that if you have a course, you have a basis for knowing where you want to be at every step along the way. That then gives rise to the opportunity to detect departures from the best course early before you are far offtrack and the waste is great. You see, Patrick, the best pilots are not ones who can nail a large, aggressive maneuver back from way out of position or off course. The best pilots are the ones who detect deviation the moment it happens, and they can apply a small correction at that instant. It looks like they never deviated at all."

"I get it. Same applies in many parts of life and business." The light was turning on for me.

"Yes. The art form here is to plan well enough that you know what the proper course to completion looks like and you are then set to see departures from that course much sooner. It has proven to be a powerful advantage to me personally in all types of endeavors."

"Thanks," I said tapping the three-by-five card. "So, sticking to the plan, what's the next lesson?"

"Pilot versus passenger."

"Pilot versus passenger? What's that? It is not on the list."

"Think of an airliner cruising on one of life's journeys. Who's calling the shots? Obviously the pilot in command has the ultimate responsibility for where the airliner goes, how it gets there, and all of the many factors and choices that must be managed along the way. Those who are sitting in the back reading their magazines are turning over those aspects of the experience to another person. That's the way many people live their lives. So many people look to others for their direction. Their lives are driven by the inbox—the opinions of others and their input from many different sources. The ones who determine to be the pilots of their own lives take full responsibility. They determine where they are going, how they are going to get there, and what they will do to manage the resources, the threats, and the opportunities along the way."

"I'm a pilot, for sure," I said. My BlackBerry buzzed. I looked down and scrolled through the text message. Nothing urgent.

"The passengers' mentality focuses on other people. They look to take from others and fill what is empty within themselves. But that is a flawed strategy. It does not work in the long haul. The emptiness that remains automatically becomes 'their' fault. It can happen in any aspect of life, and it is very subtle. Of course, you can't have it both ways. You cannot be the passenger for the bad things that happen and the pilot for the good. Most people are tempted to do that, me included, but it is very limiting and ultimately damaging."

I nodded.

"Patrick, it seems to me that your life is driven by the activity of others. As much as you like to think you're the boss of it, that you're solely focused on your business, you really aren't."

"But I am. I'm the pilot. I call the shots. I'm a born leader."

"You are a reactor, like most people. You can't even sit and have breakfast without responding to incoming text messages. And I'm your top prospect. I can imagine how you were with Hannah."

I stared at him. The BlackBerry vibrated in my jacket pocket.

"Responding to text messages makes me a passenger?"

"Not quite. But letting others distract and interrupt a scheduled one-hour meeting? Yes, I'd say that makes you a passenger. An unintentional one."

"Al, were you a pilot at some point, I mean, an actual aircraft pilot?"

"Why Patrick, what would give you that idea?"

"You sure know a lot about aviation."

He grinned. "Yes. I spent some time in the military,

and many of my analogies and ways of looking at things come from that experience. I find it to be a simplifying framework for applying principles I've discovered."

"You just get more awesome every week."

"That's good, Patrick. It's important to be awesome," he said jokingly.

"So how can I be a pilot 100 percent of the time?"

"Just make a decision to be one. Be intentional in all you do."

"But pilots have to be trained, don't forget."

Al sat back and smiled. "One classroom might be a humble diner in the inner city in Boston. Do you think you might wish to enroll in pilot training?"

"I think I already have."

Crafton checked his watch. "Are we on for next Tuesday?"

"Absolutely," I said, nodding. "But I have a suggestion. Let's meet at my place."

Crafton stopped, leaned back. His eyes narrowed. "You mean your office?"

I nodded. "Goodwin and Meyer. It's in the State Street Building just a block and a half from your office."

"Don't you think it's premature to meet there? I mean, I knew you would get pressure to show your trophy, but I don't think it helps your firm in the goal to win Castle Investments as a client. Where is the pressure coming from? Carter?"

I nodded.

"Summarize your view of your boss for me, Patrick."

"Well, he's about 42, an EVP, and he runs the best department at Goodwin and Meyer. He has moved fast and is rising further. John is a great presenter, and he does amazing work with clients. We get along well, he works hard, almost as hard as I do."

"Tell me about the man, Patrick. What kind of person is he inside?"

"He's my boss, Al. I didn't hire him. I don't need to know what kind of man he is inside. I just need to know how to make him happy."

"But now you're trying to get me to meet with him. You'll have me over, and Carter will happen to stop by. Isn't that right?"

"It sure would do me a favor."

Crafton shook his head. "Patrick, if you could pick one partner to go into a situation where the bullets would be flying and your life would likely depend on each other, would you pick Carter?"

"I don't think I know him well enough personally to answer that."

"Patrick, you know what you know. Decide. Is Carter your partner with your butt on the line or not?"

"Probably not, it's just intuition though, just a feeling. Not much to go on."

"That's a lot to go on. Pay attention to it and guard yourself. My impression is that Carter is out for himself only."

I exhaled. "So, is that a no?"

"Look, I advise against it, but if you need me to come to your office, I will, but it will need to be Wednesday. We can have our normal weekly meeting in your office, behind closed doors. I'll shake hands with your boss if you want, but make sure he knows I'm not interested in a business meeting."

"Got it. What's my assignment for next week?"

"No prep is needed. Just bring your head, heart, and ears."

We said our good-byes, and on the drive across town I dictated my report to Carter in a long voice mail. I stressed that Al Crafton had advised against a business meeting at this time. It would be premature, I said, and I told Carter that we should wait, but I thought progress was being made.

Carter left me a reply message two hours later.

"I understand," he said. "But if you can get Crafton to meet formally, we'll put our best foot forward."

I went back to my office and confirmed the meeting, and the next afternoon when I saw Carter, he told me the higher-ups were very pleased and impressed with the two of us.

FIVE

I STRAIGHTENED THE CHAIRS in my office and circled the desk again, making sure everything on the wall was lined up perfectly, my college degree in a dark cherrywood frame, the Banker of the Year award I received my third year (the youngest recipient ever), the photo of me racing cars at the Goodwin and Meyer conference in Palm Springs, and my favorite picture of all with Salma Hayek's hand on my shoulder after she signed autographs at the event. At 8:25 Stacy stepped in.

"Hurry, he's here. They've sent him up." I split for the elevator on my floor to meet Al Crafton.

The week leading up to this meeting had been intense. We put our best thinking to work to sell Al in the limited time he had given us. In the meeting at the diner the week before, Crafton had said that the total time allotted would be 90 minutes and he wanted 60 of it with me for our private conversation.

After some debate, John Carter had decided that we would keep the team to just three. Carter and our most senior officer, Patricia Redmond, waited in the conference room. Patricia was to give a brief overview of GM's capabilities and some of our victories in Al's industry. Then we would present the outlines of two attractive acquisition candidates. Carter had said that no one else had this information about the companies. I wondered how he knew that.

I arrived just before the elevator doors opened, and Al Crafton stepped out looking sharp and relaxed.

"Patrick, it's good to see you again." His smile was warm.

"Thank you for coming, Al. I know that you are doing me a personal favor meeting me here and allowing for a short presentation."

"No problem, Patrick. You stressed to John Carter and the others that I felt a business discussion at this time might be premature, right?"

I nodded. "Absolutely. Yes, I did."

"What's the game plan then?"

"If you'll follow me, we'll head to the executive conference room. We'll have a few minutes with my associates, and then we'll spend a full hour visiting in my office, as you requested."

Al nodded and we made the short trek in silence.

After brief greetings, we got right down to business and stayed on track, performing better than we had in our two dress rehearsals. Patricia was crisp and brief with her welcome and overview, and John Carter was brilliant, presenting the first candidate. I felt very good about my presentation of the leading opportunity as well. Even though he was given every chance, Al asked no questions, but he did make a brief note three times and thoughtfully nodded four times, by my count. He seemed engaged and pleasant.

"Do you have any questions on the presentation or anything we covered?" I asked. Carter smiled. Redmond sat up straight in her chair.

"Yes," Crafton said slowly. "I do. A general one."

We all leaned in. The room was quiet except for the hum of the air handlers, which I had never noticed before. I remembered a lesson from one of my sales trainers. He said that for a sales professional, questions are your friends.

"Do you have a published code of ethics for the firm, and can you tell me a little about any related training you offer?" he asked.

I glanced at Carter. He was looking at Patricia.

"About half the staff are lawyers and CPAs who get that training as part of their required continuing education," she answered smoothly. "My senior staff and I emphasize it with the rest. Is there a special reason you ask?"

"I can assure you," Carter said, jumping in before Al could respond, "that we are one of the most ethical companies you will ever work with."

After an awkward silence, Al simply nodded. "Okay," he dismissed.

Carter jumped in. "Then, I propose that Castle Investments enter into a nondisclosure agreement to allow Goodwin and Meyer to proceed with further investigation of the two acquisition opportunities."

"I can't do that," Al said evenly. "My evaluation team is absorbed and fully engaged at this time. It would be six weeks or more before we would have the capacity to take on any additional workload."

Carter challenged, "You have the reputation of always being interested in exceptional opportunities. Certainly both of these targets meet that definition based on our preliminary work, don't they?"

Al was steady. "Thanks for that compliment, John, and yes, we want to grow Castle with the right types of business combinations, and at first blush they look good, but we also play for the long term. We consider our team's health and home life. I told Patrick this discussion was premature, and I'm pretty sure he explained that to you, didn't he, John?"

Carter's eyes shot to Patricia briefly, then flicked back to Crafton.

"Not really, but I understand your position," Carter said. "And I thank you for your time today." His body language turned stiff.

"It was great to see you again, Al," Patricia said, attempting a warm smile. "When your timing is right, we will be ready." She looked my way. "Is there anything further you need from me, Patrick?" she asked.

"No, thank you," I said sheepishly.

We all stood, and Patricia Redmond and John Carter left the conference room. Crafton settled back into his chair. "How do you think that went?" he asked.

"Not so great. Carter threw me under the bus."

Crafton watched me closely. "Patrick, I know you want my business. I'm sorry I couldn't sign the nondisclosure agreement. It would have been a short-term expedient, but overall dishonest, as I have no current intention of being a client of your firm based on my present impression. I won't lead them on."

"I told John you weren't ready," I said.

"I know."

"I allowed them to maneuver you into an ambush," I admitted. "I'm sorry."

"Human beings are progressive at the core, Patrick. We all want to move things forward, and sometimes we push hard to do that even when it's not in our own best interest."

Al put his hands on the table in front of him. "See, for some reason humans 'require' continuous advancement. As long as we have breath, we are not satisfied with the status quo. We're always looking for more or better. It is a universal trait, a design feature. I believe such design features are there for a reason. In this case, the fact that we are progressive in our nature is like the curve in the boomerang. It causes us to keep turning back to home, so to speak, in a continuous search for real truth and purpose. We're not satisfied until we find it."

I keyed his points into my BlackBerry. "I'm taking notes," I said, "not sending text messages. Is this our weekly pilot training session?"

Crafton smiled. "If you're ready."

"I'm ready." I was relieved to quit talking about the meeting.

"Let me give you a couple of examples of why I say all of us are very progressive. Did you notice when you were between 85 and 95 percent through college, working toward your degree, that your mind automatically started reaching beyond graduation, thinking seriously about 'what's next'? It's a good and natural thing, and it is absolutely unavoidable. Until that point, your focus was almost completely on the work at hand, getting your degree, a major accomplishment."

"Yes, that happened to me. But that's life," I said.

"Of course. But progression can be like a runaway train. It can be negative, if you let it. Look at alcoholism or drug abuse, for instance. If two drinks or two drug doses satisfy this week, it will likely take three next week, four the next, and so on. The way human beings look to satisfy themselves always requires more and more. It is universal in all people. So, be thoughtful where you put your effort when you go seeking real satisfaction."

"Al, this is making sense. Are we back to the subject of target fixation?"

"Yes and no. Target fixation applies to one goal or focus area. Our progressive nature applies to our entire personal value system," Al gestured with a horizontal motion, palm down, symbolizing all parts of us.

"Okay, I see how it fits."

"It's all life," he said. "If a person truly sells out to accomplish a major objective and ignores balance in the process, he or she will invariably find that any satisfaction is short lived, even if he or she accomplishes the objective. We often hear of people who perform at the very top of their field for a time, but then they lose their balance, fall from the perch, and are sadly miserable thereafter. We all have a next big thing we are working toward and we think about. Then, when we are almost there, our mind reaches beyond and begins to develop the new next big thing."

"Yup. I see what you mean."

"It's not a bad thing; just recognize that it is the way we are wired. Accept this design feature of yourself, and use it for positive progress."

"I get that."

"Before we move on, let me stress an earlier point. As we discussed, the desire for progression operates negatively too if we plug in the wrong source of satisfaction . . . like food, drugs, alcohol, fame, pleasure, influence, physical fitness, religion, love, beauty, et cetera. It takes more and more and more to temporarily satisfy the deepest desires and legitimate needs of our hearts. So be careful what you plug in there. The world says those things will make you happy if you can just get enough of them. In our world, those 'routes to joy' are found in greatest concentration in the Hollywood crowd, and yet you'd be hard-pressed to find a group of people more dissatisfied and dysfunctional."

I nodded, "The Hollywood list . . . it's a lie then?"

"Yes, but so is keeping up with the Joneses." He stood and walked to the whiteboard, looking for a marker. He found a blue one and drew a large triangle.

"I don't think I've ever seen anyone use that board before," I said.

"Here's an illustration," Crafton said. "Carter is your boss, and you have seemed to hold him in regard, which probably meant in the past that you'd go the extra mile for him. Would you agree?"

"In the past, yes. But not now. That changed a few minutes ago, the moment he turned on me and lied about the facts."

Crafton seemed contemplative. He smiled. "Patrick, let's look at it from his perspective." He drew an X at the top of the triangle as he said, "Carter is up here." He drew another X in the bottom right corner of the triangle. "You're here. So what did Carter win or lose today?"

"He hurt his chances of ever making you a client. He lost some ground with his boss, and in trying to limit that damage, he lied about me. As a result, he has lost my trust and loyalty."

"That's true, but he's still here, right?" Crafton tapped the top of the triangle with the marker.

"Yes."

"Now roll the video and you can see that no matter how it plays out exactly—you stay, you go, you get promoted past him, no matter—things are fundamentally changed for you but not for him or the firm's corporate culture."

"Roll the video?"

"Yes, mature people are able to see shorter-term events and choices in the context of longer-term effects. We can all envision the future. 'Roll the video' is the term I use to remind myself to look forward."

"I see."

"Immaturity tempts us to look only at the immediate reward, but we need to think beyond to the longer-term cost or effect. Think about balance, then decide."

"Okay, as I roll the video, I see Carter still here," I offered.

"Yes, and he's still going to have the same values. He's not going to change. And he's still going to be king of the jungle, so to speak. Up here at the top of the triangle."

He erased it all and sat down in the chair in front of me. "The point is that only you can live your own, authentic life. It's up to you to change, and live by new values. None of us can separate our basic values and beliefs from who we are. It shows up in all aspects of life, including the workplace. If you want career success, don't work too much on how to portray things on the surface. Remember integrity and what it is. Work mostly on who you really are, because over time that will come through loud and clear to others. That is the business application of the points we have been discussing since we met."

Al hesitated, as if he was waiting for dawn to break on my understanding.

"That's big," I said.

"Integrity is being the same on the inside as you are on the outside, and that applies to organizations as well as people, doesn't it? So you have to remember to be real. But don't apply this as a standard of perfection. No human is perfect. We all fail at times and disappoint each other and ourselves. I do find, however, a very large difference between those who thoughtfully try to choose and follow the better path and those who either have not thought about it or find the apparent shortcuts too tempting."

"I had not thought about entire organizations as having or not having integrity. You are talking about the culture here, aren't you?"

"Not just here, but everywhere. If I could leave you on this planet with just one lesson, it would be to live with integrity, which means being authentic at all times. With yourself, with peers, with clients, and in all your relationships. That's a huge part of leadership."

"It's hard to be authentic when you feel like you have to perform a role in corporate America," I said. "It's a fight to win."

"But that's being a leader. A real leader. A transparent, authentic leader. People like to be around someone authentic. They can tell. Leadership is a mindset, and it's also set of skills that can definitely be learned. You're not born a leader; that's a myth. If I have skill in that area, it is all learned, for sure," he said.

"How do you learn to lead?"

"Patrick, that depends on what you consider to be the role of the leader."

"I'd say to provide direction," I replied, pretty satisfied with my answer.

"I accept that, but let's unpack that thought. How does the leader know which way to direct?"

"By rolling the video?" I guessed.

"Yes, but from a higher vantage point. One that's gained only by rising above everyone else."

"How?"

"True leadership has many facets, but it begins with the need to see more and see farther than those being led. Sometimes you have to see the invisible. The leader who is not a step ahead is not effective because a person cannot lead from behind. So my internal reminder is to continually 'rise above' in my mind's eye to see the broader picture. I use the image of a helicopter over a battlefield to help me."

"Okay, that resonates, but it also seems pretty obvious."

"Yes, it is obvious while we are sitting here, but it's harder to remember when the bullets are flying. It must become a matter of discipline and practice."

I nodded, "I once heard an old saying about that. When you are up to your elbows in alligators, it is hard to remember you are there to drain the swamp."

"Patrick, next question: Who decides who the leader is?" he asked.

"Not sure what you mean, Al."

"There are various levels of commitment and energy, creativity and focus, depth and texture that humans bring to any task. A great team has its members working from deep within themselves for the good of the whole. This level of commitment really reduces the interpersonal friction, too. Bottom line: The followers decide who the leader is. If they are willing to follow and to bring more and more of what they have to offer to the team, greater things will happen. Interestingly, even if you are the designated leader, but you have no one following . . ."

"Right, I am leading no one," I summarize.

"Patrick, most people just won't do the hard work. You've said that over and over. The pack ends up less successful, less effective, and less satisfied. Don't be satisfied following the pack. Even a dead fish can swim with the current, you know."

I laughed.

"Lastly, remember that you are not always the leader. None of us is. Sometimes we are in the follower role. It has dignity too. We are all under authority."

"Okay," I nodded.

"So be a great follower when you are in that role. Be thoughtful and supportive. Give honest feedback, especially when you think the leader is missing something, but be respectful. Accept and support her decisions or get off the team. Being a great follower will help you grow as a leader."

Suddenly the image of the beautiful girl in the white gauze dress popped into my head. I hadn't been a very good leader in keeping the relationship together. I hadn't been a good provider in any sense, except financial.

As I walked Al to the elevator, we agreed to meet at his office the following week.

"Don't lose any sleep about the meeting today," Crafton said. "I understand."

"Thanks, Al. That helps a lot. Sorry about the ambush."

SIX

THE FOLLOWING WEEK, before the meeting at Al's office, I sat on the barstool at the granite counter in my kitchen, staring into my coffee cup. It was early. Since his office was only two blocks from mine, I had planned to grab an hour at my desk before the session with Al, but I couldn't seem to get my mind off of what had happened with Hannah the night before.

It was supposed to be a casual dinner to catch up and move ahead on the divorce, but two hours later we were still talking. She was always such a patient listener, and I had a lot to tell her. But I was surprised by the way I felt when I saw her again. I was excited just to be with her. Then at the end of the dinner, she said something that sent me reeling.

"Patrick," she said, "I'm seeing someone."

I had no right to care, but it was like a blow to my midsection. I had never considered the possibility. My Hannah? Seeing someone?

I didn't sleep all night. On the way to Castle Investments a phrase kept rolling over in my mind . . . things are not always as they seem. Just two months ago I was the rising star at Goodwin and Meyer, free of the encumbrances of wife and children and on the fast track to my goals. I had the world by the tail. Now I was questioning everything. What was it all for?

John Carter had been distant for the past week, probably not sure he wanted to face me after what he did. But yesterday he called me in and was steadfast in his demand that I get Crafton on track toward client status with Goodwin and Meyer. He had pressed me for a strategy, but I didn't have one. We simply couldn't push a man like Crafton. Even if we could, I wouldn't. Not again.

"The reason Crafton wants to meet with me has nothing to do with the firm," I explained.

"You're trying to tell me that Al Crafton simply wants to meet with you, Patrick, just to be . . . to be your friend? Come on."

I glared at John Carter across the table. It's you he doesn't like, I wanted to say. Mentioning our business proposal in any way to Al would make me look and feel extremely shallow and selfish . . . plain and simple. But Carter wasn't listening.

I was running 15 minutes early for the meeting at Crafton's office, so I stopped at the corner stand for a shoeshine, mindful of the dramatic shift in my motives for continuing to meet with him. Two months ago it was 95 percent business opportunity and 5 percent whatever else he had to offer. Now the needle was shifting and I really was interested.

I walked into Castle Investments and stopped at the imposing reception desk. The security guard looked into a row of small monitors with a view of people streaming in and out of the elevator bank.

"Name?" the guard asked.

"Patrick Mitchell. I'm here to see Al Crafton."

I was watching for a reaction when I mentioned the CEO's name, but he didn't seem to care. The guard dialed the telephone. He surveyed me quickly, handing over a badge. "Wear this at all times, and return it to me when you leave the building," he said. He pushed a sheet of lined paper in front of me and pointed to it. I signed in. "Someone will be right with you."

I walked over and stared out the windows, looking across State Street at the rusty modern metal sculpture mounted there. Then I turned around and surveyed. The lobby was impressive. I wondered what Crafton's office would look like.

"Mr. Mitchell?" A woman, maybe 60, approached. Her gray hair was pulled back into a tight style, and she wore an elegant blue suit with shiny gold buttons.

"I'm Terry Alden," she said, extending her hand. "Mr. Crafton's assistant." She gestured toward the elevators. "Shall we?"

I nodded and followed her past the elevator bank and around a corner to an unmarked door. She used her badge on the security sensor and opened the door, beckoning me to walk through. On the other side was a small room with its own elevator. Ms. Alden was quick with her badge once again until we were on our way to the top floor, bypassing the masses. Nice perk.

"Have you worked here long?" I asked, the elevator rising.

"Twenty-seven years and two months. Over twenty-four working directly for Mr. Crafton." She paused, surveying me briefly. "You are a fortunate young man. Mr. C. has a real interest in you."

"He's a great guy," I said, "Does Al meet with many like me?"

"A small handful over the years. One at a time."

The elevator hit 72, and we stepped out.

"Terry, why does Al spend time with guys like me?" She stopped and turned.

"You're arrows into the future. He wants to help the arrows fly straight and true. At least that's how he describes it," she mused. "Mr. Crafton offers extra attention only to those people he believes will make the most of what he has to offer. He says he finds the greatest potential in people at opposite ends of life's situational spectrum. Have you been to HOPE Center?"

I nodded.

"Mr. C. believes in offering opportunity. He helped found the center years ago, and has remained fully involved. It changes lives, Patrick. Consistent and dramatic life change. That's what it's all about." She pointed at my chest. "But Mr. C. believes the greater opportunity is at your end of the scale. You are a talented and motivated younger person with unlimited potential. Many more lives can be touched over time by accelerating the life lessons you'd probably eventually learn anyway."

"How long does Al usually meet with his 'arrows'?" I wondered out loud.

"It varies considerably. He is willing to spend the time and effort as long as there is hunger for more and a real effort to grow. His goal is to accelerate the growth process, for you and the dozens of people you touch. Why wait until you're in the final semester to do something great?"

I thought about my dad. "Some people don't make it to 60," I said.

"You're right. There's no guarantee."

She turned and walked down the corridor until we reached Al's quiet, corner office. It was simple, with loam-colored walls and dark wood trim. A tray of bagels and cream cheese, cut fruit, and coffee were arrayed in the center of the conference table near one of the two window walls. Al was nowhere to be seen, but Terry ushered me right in.

"He'll be here soon," she said.

The office was plenty roomy and well appointed, but I had expected more in the way of luxury. It was under-stated, tasteful, and functional. There was a desk with a side return for visitors' convenience, a good-sized conver-sation area, and a conference table with six chairs. The fur-niture was all coordinated and interchangeable. It seemed that extra attention had been paid to the lighting. Each part of the office was washed in warm illumination, but there was enhanced lighting for the three subspaces and the decorating accents. A door built into the sidewall panel opened and Al stepped in. The corner office came com-plete with a corner washroom.

"Patrick, welcome. How are you?"

"Hi, Al. I'm great."

"Let's sit, hope you are hungry. This is not the gourmet fare we get at Fred's, and we don't get to see Marge, but maybe we can make do."

We munched on bagels and fruit, and I looked at the framed photos on a low table at the end of the leather sofa. A black-and-white 8-by-10 showed two young men in military flight suits and vests with lots of bulging pockets standing in front of a big, serious-looking jet. I pointed to it with my fork.

"That a plane you flew?"

"Yup, over 1,500 hours, about half in combat."

"What kind of aircraft?"

"That's the workhorse of its day, the F-4 Phantom II."

"Looks fast."

"It was in some versions, the ones where speed really mattered, like Recon. The saying was that the F-4 proved you could take a barn supersonic with big enough engines. Those were big engines."

"Who's that with you?"

"His name was Robert Ramsey Madison, nickname 'Railroad'! He was my best friend in the early years. A southern boy who talked slow and thought fast. Distinguished graduate from the Air Force Academy and tops in his pilot training class. A magnificent man, wound tighter than a yo-yo. He saved my life one afternoon with a spot-on radio call. He had a split second to let me know that an inexperienced lieutenant in the formation was about to collide from my blind side underneath. He used two words, 'lead breakout,' and they were perfect. I immediately knew what was happening and what to do. I avoided a big midair collision." Al was quiet, and far away. I respected the moment and remained silent.

"Wish I could have returned the favor a few years later," he said.

I remembered what Al's driver said he had been doing on that San Francisco trip. His friend had died; I wondered if there was more to it.

"Railroad has a son?" I asked.

"Yes, Tim, and a daughter, Raney. Wonderful kids . . . well, not kids now because they're in their late thirties. How'd you know about Tim?"

"The night we met I talked briefly with your driver, Anthony, at Logan. He told me you were visiting the son of a good friend who was. . .who had . . . uh . . ." I tried to be delicate.

"Committed suicide. You can say it. It happened. Saddest day ever for me. I was shocked, devastated, sad and angry, but mostly remorseful. I had deep regret that Railroad was suffering so much and I didn't pick up on it. After that, I committed every fiber in me to learn all I could to be able to help people."

"Why did he kill himself?"

"He missed it and spun in."

"Missed what?"

"He did not maintain aircraft control, so to speak. He was a great pilot, sure, but in the end he missed all of these life lessons we've been talking about. He got totally out of balance and went into the emotional equivalent of what aviators call a 'graveyard spiral.' You should look that up. It can happen when a pilot does not believe his instruments and goes instead on what it feels like the airplane is doing. You get vertigo and literally don't know which way is up. Then the harder you try, the worse you make things." Al stared out the window.

"Don't we all get vertigo once in a while?" I asked.

"Yes, it's possible. It revolves around our most fundamental need, hope. We can live some weeks without food. Days without water and minutes without air. But if we lose hope, we're done."

"Never heard it put like that."

"Hope is simply a reasonable expectation for a brighter tomorrow. Lose that, and you lose it all. Of course, the choices we make form our basis for hope or lack of it. It's pilot versus passenger again."

"When we spiral, it's time to recognize it and apply careful correction, right?"

"Yes. We all get vertigo. But if we live in our emotions and don't have any belief that there's more than just what we can see right in front of us, it's hard, sometimes impossible, to get out of the spin. We claim truth with our minds, not our hearts. We should be aware of feelings, not ignore or suppress them, but we should not be ruled by them either. Choice is the outcome of thinking. But some people just stay stuck in the spiral, wasting potential at the minimum, and hitting the ground hard at the max."

Al stood and closed his office door. He walked back to the table, took a bite of a bagel.

"That's amazing!" I said.

"What?"

"How you synthesize things."

"A commitment to simple, powerful principles and years of experience, Patrick. So tell me what's going on at the firm?"

"Nothing new."

"Carter still driving you hard?"

"Actually quieter this week than last. Maybe he doesn't have the guts to face me. He did try to put me on the grill yesterday." I laughed. "Of course, I've been his golden boy up until now. So this is new. He doesn't think I'm doing enough to get your business. He wants me to make it happen."

"And if you don't?"

I shrugged. "I have seen him fire for less. Something's different. It's unfair. You were square with me on your viewpoint, and I was very careful to keep Carter aware.

He knew it all, but when his boss was there and you asked outright if I had kept him informed, he lied. Apparently one of us had to look bad, so he picked me. I think he made too many promises to Patricia Redmond. It is important to me that you know I never told him you'd sign his nondisclosure agreement."

"Patrick, when Redmond first took over Goodwin and Meyer in Boston, she made me a project for several months. She tried several times to get the GM foot in the door here, but I wanted to see if the new leader would have a positive effect on that team before I would say yes."

"What happened?"

"After many months and failed attempts, Patricia called and just asked outright if there was anything she could do to win our business. I told her no, not at that time nor in the foreseeable future. She went away."

"Actually, Al, I had heard that story."

"Okay then, rise above, roll the video, and put the picture together. You know how Carter is wired and how much he wants to get ahead. When there was a chance he could get Castle as a client firm, he could not resist telling Redmond that it was happening. She came to our meeting probably thinking it was a done deal. Carter was in essence saying to her . . . 'look, you failed, but I'm getting it done. I am better than you, promote me.'"

I nodded.

"Let's say that I was willing to do a deal with Goodwin and Meyer just to help you. It is your call to make: Do I do it? Yes or no?"

"You'd be willing to do that?" I was amazed.

"Apply your training. You could be unfairly terminated by your boss just because you couldn't get a client that he's promising his boss and because you won't play by his rules and pressure me to work with your firm. A few days ago you were the rising star. Right now you may be hiding it, but you have to be scared, angry, and hurt. Be aware of your heart, but process my question in your head. Think it through. Now, I did not say I would be willing to become a client to save you. I may or may not. My question was rhetorical. I said 'Let's say that I was willing . . .' Would you have me do it?"

I stared at him. Get out of my heart and into my head.

"Okay, I think I get it. You want me to roll the video beyond the obvious, short-term solution, right? If I say yes to your offer, you become a client. But you've already said you don't fit with our culture, and you don't like Carter."

Al pressed, "But you have believed in your firm, and you know how hard you are willing to work. So you could be selling me based on your honest beliefs."

I pondered his statement. It was true. I did believe in the firm, at times. I also believed that Crafton was right about a lot of things. I looked around his office. Everything felt different. Even the people who worked there were different. Slower, nicer, more relaxed.

"Al, I can see what you have meant about the difference in the cultures of Castle and GM. I don't think there is a basis for a good long-term partnership, so it would be short sighted, or worse yet selfish, for me to ask you to do this favor. So I'd say no."

"Good answer," he said. "Because culturally, it's not a fit."

We both sat comfortably silent for a long moment as Al let me digest.

"How is your culture different?" I wanted his view.

"Our culture is centered on our core values, whereas most corporate cultures are centered on profit and productivity. Everything we do is driven by a strong value system. We focus on it, we talk about values, and we hold each other to those standards. And I don't hire people who don't fit well within our culture."

"And you don't do business with companies that don't fit with your culture."

"That's right, Patrick. Not for a significant relationship anyway. Trust has two parts. Do you trust motives, and do you trust judgment and ability? Say no to either, no trust. I have learned if you work with trustworthy people, you can work out any problem. If you deal with untrustworthy people, you can't write enough down in contracts to protect yourself. You have to have standards, and once you have real clarity on what they are, it becomes much easier to act in accord with them. That, in a nutshell, is the basis of Castle's success."

"If you did business with my firm, I think you'd lose respect for me. It might be a short-term win, but you'd lose respect because too many of our people are more or less like Carter. I just can't say it's a good fit for you right now."

"But one day it might be, especially if you're running the firm. You'd make some real changes. Patrick, I am very proud of you. This is not an academic exercise but a rare real-life lesson opportunity. There are no accidents. You are getting it right."

SEVEN

"So, this place is growing on you?" Crafton smiled wide, like a kid in a candy store. He slid into the booth at Fred's and reached across, punching me on the shoulder playfully. "Are you ready to admit that Fred's is becoming your favorite restaurant?"

"Not quite," I said.

Marge walked over with coffee and menus. An attached card announced that the special of the day was "Eggs Benedict, Texas Style."

"What does 'Texas Style' mean?" I asked.

"That just means it's big," she said. "Three eggs."

"I'll have that then," I said, "and I'll consider it lunch too."

"I'll have the usual," Crafton said, smiling at Marge.

"Small eggbeater omelet with lotsa ham and a little cheese, tomatoes on the side, dry whole wheat toast. Coming up."

She walked toward the grill area and shouted to the guys over the counter. "One AC! One Texas Benedict."

"AC? Is that the Al Crafton special? You have a breakfast plate named after you? Wow, I am not worthy. I guess that gives me a framework for knowing when I arrive."

Crafton smiled, sipped his coffee. His eyes twinkled. "Sorry, my friend. You haven't made it until they actually print it on the menu. I have a ways to go before Fred commits fonts."

"I do like this place," I admitted. "Food's great, and it's unpretentious."

"Is that Patrick Mitchell I hear?"

"Ha. You're a comedian."

"I'm glad you are starting to like it. Meeting here simplifies my Tuesday schedule. I am already near HOPE Center when we finish. That gives us a few extra minutes together, which I value."

I had a flashback to a Saturday my dad wanted to take my football team to lunch after our middle school game. We had just won our third game of the season and we piled into the old wagon to go to lunch, with several cars and parents following. I was eager to impress my teammates, and dad drove us straight to a dive for lunch. A total greasy spoon! I was mortified. I figured he could at least afford a nice restaurant, but he said if he was paying, he got to choose where we went. Crafton was a lot like my dad. He did not care much about appearances. Maybe I was too.

"Not a problem, Omelet Al. My new name for you since all you pilots have nicknames."

Marge swung by with our plates. "Anything else you boys need?"

We shook our heads.

"So update me on your work situation," Crafton said.

"Carter has been out of the office a lot since we last met, and that's been nice. Last Friday he called me and we talked for about 30 minutes. Things were a bit tense, but we didn't talk about his false report to Patricia. It's like a hand grenade in the room. Nobody wants to acknowledge it, much less pull the pin. But I had an epiphany last night. Listen to this: Goodwin and Meyer has a leading-edge phone system. Voice mails that go into the system are kept in digital files for something like two years. There are several voice mail messages that will prove Carter is the liar and I played it straight up. Bet he hasn't thought of that."

"Slow down. You're talking too fast. What do you mean?"

"After one of our meetings, Carter was on the road, so I left him a full report on voice mail, including what you had told me about eventually giving Goodwin and Meyer a chance, but that it was premature at that time. I must have talked five or six minutes. I even quoted you about the 'steep hill to climb' and me being the best chance."

"You are sure those messages are retained?"

"Absolutely. I think they are even stored off site. Carter answered with a voice mail in which he said he understood. He said we had to sell the appointment first. Keep at it. It was his decision and his risk. He said something about blowing through your smokescreen. Maybe I should not have told you that part—sorry."

"Not a problem, strictly between us, it's not like you'll damage my deep respect for his character."

"I can nail him to the wall with these messages, or at least put one torpedo in him below the waterline."

Al sat for a moment, sipping his coffee. "Patrick, have you ever tried to put toothpaste back in the tube because you squeezed too much out?"

"Can't say I have. Sounds almost impossible to do."

"It is, which is precisely the point. Some actions in life are undoable once you pull the trigger. When you recognize that you have one of those situations at hand, be thoughtful and careful. There are some very specific considerations that help you decide what to do."

"Ok, like what?"

"Consider timing of the action. You rarely have to make the call right away, so take whatever time you do have and get in close touch with your highest desires for all involved. Take a day to think about important things like this. Understand your own intentions. The other question then to ask yourself is, 'What is the best, most redemptive thing I can do for the greatest number of people?' You should not move too quickly on an action that has negative outcomes for anyone until you have rolled over those questions in your mind. Once you've done that, you can make the right decision. Consider the paths you can choose and the probable, longer-term outcome of each one, both for you and for other people. Then pick."

"You mean you think I shouldn't take those voice mails straight to Patricia Redmond this morning? Am I hearing you right?"

"All I am saying is that once you do it, you cannot undo it, smooth everything over, and live happily ever after."

I stared into his blue eyes, which seemed gray at certain moments.

"So, roll the video in your mind. If you think the outcome makes the action attractive, make sure you are doing it for the right reason, not just taking care of some need or desire of your own. Ask yourself, 'What is the most beneficial thing I can do to help as many as possible, long term?' Include yourself in that, but not exclusively. Those are the lenses to look through when making this decision. Roll the video forward. Think about how it will affect your life, his life, and the lives of the others around him."

I surveyed the diner, exhaled. The place was littered with the same crowd. A few guys on stools at the counter, and a couple of workers were getting fueled up at the tables against the wall.

"He'd get fired," I said.

"And his family?"

"He'd find another job."

"Just consider and weigh as many aspects of your contemplated action as possible."

"Yes. Okay, I get it. I'll think about it."

"That's the point. Think about it. Patrick, it seems like you've been a high performer all your life."

I nodded. I had been. It was true.

"A lot of people who are high performers come from challenging backgrounds. They've had some sort of dysfunction or tragedy, like alcoholism in their family. Did you have any of that?"

"No, definitely not."

"So you're a high performer by your own choosing. Just caught up in the chase, the game of life, that it?"

"I suppose so. Is that bad? I mean, from where I sit, your bio does not contain the word 'slouch.' You're a high performer if there ever was one."

Crafton laughed.

I went on, "I suppose we could turn all of these questions around and ask you the same thing. Did your dog die when you were 10, causing you to go out and build one of the most successful companies in the world?"

Crafton grinned. He shook his head. "Patrick, my friend, you're a piece of work."

"Until I met you, I figured some people just get it, and most don't," I said. "I thought it could be boiled down to that kind of simplicity."

"What do you mean?" Crafton asked.

"I mean that some people are successful in life and in business, and some aren't. Some just get it, like you do, and like I do, but most don't."

"So you think you get it, do you?" His face was serious now.

"Well, I used to think I was responsible for all of my success, and yes, I used to think I 'got it' all of the time. I'm the top rookie in my firm, on track to be the youngest to make partner while some of my peers have been trudging along in there for 20 years and will never make partner." I motioned Marge over for more coffee. "But now you have shown me that there are other things I've missed."

"So you're open to learning now."

"Thanks to you."

Crafton lowered his head. "I hope I've been helpful. Some days it's hard to tell. So where do you see yourself in 10 years?"

"I see myself running a successful company. Just like you. But it may or may not be at Goodwin and Meyer, depending on how things play out. I could be promoted soon if my boss is let go, you know."

"Really? Is that what you want? And at all costs?" He lifted his coffee and stopped, waiting for my reply.

"That's one of your loaded questions, isn't it? 'At all costs' implies too much focus on one thing. So, no, not at all costs, but yes, at a reasonable cost. Clearly Carter is a liar who has it coming. He deserves to be poured out. I need to protect my reputation in my industry. Just considering all options here, of course, just like I promised."

"That is a point to consider, sure. But busting Carter could get you the reputation of being a hatchet man, ready to use any advantage. Think about that angle too."

"Can we change subjects?"

"Sure."

"I also see myself married in 10 years. Maybe even with kids."

Crafton hesitated. "I see. Married to just anyone?"

"I have been looking for a way to tell you that I have seen Hannah a couple of times in the last three weeks."

"Really?" His eyes lit up.

"But don't jump to conclusions. She's seeing some other guy, apparently 'a good guy,' in her words."

"Who has been the one reaching out? You or her?" Al asked.

"I called her and asked her out to dinner to discuss the divorce, but it was like a first date again. I saw her in a completely different light. And when I found out she was seeing someone else, I felt like I'd been kicked in my stomach. I was sick."

"How have you seen her differently?"

"She never supported my career in the past. I see now that I placed too much weight in one place and not the whole picture. I appeared selfish to her."

Al interrupted, "Stop, what did you say?"

I paused and thought, "Okay, I was selfish."

"Very good, go on."

"Actually, Hannah told me just a couple of days ago that I seem really different now. She asked me what had changed."

"And?"

"You, I said. I told her it was you."

"It's not me, Patrick. It's all inside you. The secret was there all along."

I shrugged. Crafton motioned for the check.

"Keep up the good work, Patrick. Next week, same time, same place?"

"Yes. The assignment?"

"Balanced living."

This time I picked up the bill and headed out last. Al was already at HOPE Center before I cranked up the BMW and headed downtown. I had a lot on my plate, but I'd decided to delay a request to see Patricia Redmond. I decided that for now, I'd let it go.

EIGHT

On Thursday I was on a conference call in my office when my personal cell chirped. It was Hannah's number. I answered right away, placing the conference call on mute.

"Hello, Hannah." I tried to mask my excitement.

"Hi, Patrick. I'm surprised you answered. I thought I might have to leave you a voice mail."

"In the last year, I don't think you've called me once," I said softly. "I wasn't going to let you leave a voice mail. It's good to hear from you."

"Are you free for lunch today?" she blurted.

"Why? What's on your mind?"

I glanced down at my schedule. I had a lunch meeting I'd have to rearrange, and a meeting with one of the other bankers just after that.

"If you're tied up, no big deal," she said, offering me an out.

"I'm free," I said quickly. "How about that sushi place just down from you at 11:30?"

She laughed. "You always hated sushi."

"I haven't had sushi in a long time. Maybe I need to try it again since you like it so much. It's light, and good for you, right?"

The line was silent.

"Hannah?"

"Excuse me, sir. I was calling Patrick Mitchell, the investment banker. What have you done with him?"

"Very funny. See you at 11:30, then?"

"Okay, Mr. California Roll!"

"Patrick, do you think you can have that analysis complete by Monday?" My name filtered through the speaker and pulled me back to earth. "Patrick?"

I put my face down within inches of the box and took it off mute. "Absolutely," I said, smiling.

———

At 11:00 I bolted from the office to meet Hannah for lunch. When she walked in a little early too, I exhaled. We talked about family news on both sides and a trip we had taken to Europe, one of the best times of our marriage. I tried the sushi, but I had also ordered a good salad just in case. Hannah noticed but said nothing.

"So how's Mr. X?" I asked.

"Excuse me?"

"You know, the dork you're dating." I smiled. "Sorry."

"Patrick, he's not a dork. He's a really nice man, who's got it all together. You'd like him."

"I assure you I wouldn't."

"We have fun together. But he's trying to move faster than I want. How are things at work?"

"Not so great. Carter and I had a falling out, so it hasn't been pleasant around there. I've kind of lost my passion for it, actually."

Her eyes widened. "Really? I can't believe I'm hearing this."

My mood had shifted. I detected hints of sadness, anger, hurt, and an undertone of dismay. I tried to remember what Crafton had said about getting into my head, and not my heart. Or was I supposed to stay in my heart? I couldn't remember here with the bullets flying.

"I thought you were the unchallenged rising star?"

I lowered my head. "I don't know, Han. I don't know anything anymore. The firm is different now. Carter and Redmond, they're not in my corner like they used to be."

"Patrick, you were sold out to that place, and I was always number 2. Lately you've seemed somehow different, and now I know why. Your number 1 priority is giving you grief, so you call in the backup for some temporary relief."

"What?"

"When the job thing settles down, you'll be the same as before." She bit her lip. "I love you, Patrick, but not enough to go through all that again."

Hannah got up and was out the door. Just like that.

I slapped two twenties on the table and went after her. She was a half block ahead, and I had her in sight. I wanted to run to her and tell her she was wrong. Convince her. But my feet wouldn't take me there. What if she was right? I stopped, feeling sick to my stomach. I turned around at the next corner and headed back to the office.

Five minutes after I sat down at my desk, Stacy came in.

"Carter wants to see you," she said.

"Now?"

She nodded. "Yes."

"Okay, thanks, Stacy."

I walked slowly to Carter's office, feeling heavier with each step.

"Where do we stand on Crafton? Any progress?" he said the minute I stepped in.

I sat down at the chair in front of his desk. "No, John, I cannot say there is, really."

Carter kept his eyes on his computer screen and typed on the keyboard, answering e-mails. "When do you think you can deliver on your promise?"

"What promise is that?"

"Mitchell, you led me to believe you could deliver Crafton, and I passed that good news up to Redmond to get the resources freed up for all that research and staff work. Redmond rescheduled a trip to Atlanta to sit in with us in that meeting the other day. You embarrassed us both, plus yourself, and you may have hurt our ultimate chances with Crafton's firm. Don't play word games with me."

"John, I have never played games with you. I feel confident that I never created any expectation that Crafton would be warm to our proposals at this time. He was clear with me, and I was clear with you." I looked him squarely in the eyes.

He glanced back down at the keyboard, and smiled. He resumed the typing. "Patrick, you are a talent, and you have done well here, but you are missing a piece or two. You lack the kill instinct. I am disappointed to tell you that you don't fit on the team at Goodwin and Meyer."

"I don't fit?"

"I'm going to have to terminate you, effective immediately."

"What?" I leaned forward. "Are you kidding me? You are firing me because you messed up, John?"

"You can point the finger only at yourself. You have to be able to deliver when the chips are on the table. You have failed. And this project could not have had higher visibility."

Carter stood, just as he had trained us to do when it was time to end a meeting and get people out of our office. If you stood, the other party would mirror your body language naturally and rise too. I stayed in the chair. "Is this who you are?" I asked. "Because I am not the one who is at fault, John. You know that, so why are you really firing me?"

"I've made my decision," he said. "Security will give you about 20 minutes, and then they'll come down to escort you out. Lori from HR is waiting in my outer office to go with you and get you to sign some release documents. I regret it came to this, and I wish you well, Patrick."

I stood, walked to the door, and turned.

"Carter, you are right, I don't fit in here."

I walked briskly to my office, the HR person following. Stacy was at her post and looked up, her eyes red.

"I'm so sorry, Patrick. I just heard the news . . ."

Man, that was fast.

I stopped and touched her arm. "Stacy, I know I haven't been great to you. I want to apologize. I'm sorry if I haven't been the best boss."

"It's okay, you've been fine . . ."

"I just want you to know how much I have appreciated working with you. You've been a rock amidst the storms around here. If I can help in any way . . ."

Stacy gave me a stiff, awkward hug just as the uniformed security officer arrived. After the papers were signed, I was escorted to the garage, then to the gate. I used my badge for the last time to open the gate, handed the badge over, and turned left on the one-way street. I had the rest of the day off.

———

When I settled in, I exhaled, and dialed Crafton's number. He answered on the first ring.

"Patrick Mitchell, to what do I owe this honor?"

"Thank God you answered," I said.

"What's wrong?"

"Is this a bad time?" I asked.

"Anthony has me headed to Marblehead, so the timing could not be better. How are you?"

"Not good. I just joined the ranks of the unemployed."

The line was silent for a second. I heard traffic in the background.

"I see. That is newsworthy. Whose initiative was it, yours or theirs?"

"Theirs—actually Carter's."

"Their loss, Patrick. But you know that. Tell me, by how many hours or days did he beat you to it? Is that a fair question?"

"I'm not sure I ever would have left on my own," I admitted.

"What shape are you really in, Patrick?"

"Shocked, but calm and steady."

"Do you have plans tonight? I would like for you to come out to Marblehead. We can talk."

"Well, let me see if I can fit you into my busy schedule."

Crafton laughed. "Look on the bright side, lots of time now!"

"Lots of time and no money," I said.

"My wife is out of town for a couple of days visiting one of the kids. Come about 6:30, and I will order up a pizza, and we'll solve all the problems of the universe, deal?"

"Deal."

He gave me the address. "Go home and kick your feet up, Patrick, or work out. Take some stress off for two or three hours."

"Thanks, Al. I would like to, but I have some planning to do. I get paid for 14 more days, and then it stops. I have a couple of credit cards not at their limit, but I have to look at everything to see if I can make it to the end of the month."

"That tight is it?"

I hadn't planned well, but I hated to admit it.

"See you soon," Al said.

————

The map I printed off the Internet took me right to the front gate of Al's section of Marblehead. It was only 6 p.m. and I had some time to kill, so I drove past the gate and looked around the area. I had been out this way about two years ago, but I didn't recall how appealing it was as a residential community with history, great views, and amazing homes. At 6:30 sharp, I had cleared security and was pulling up the noticeable incline of Al's stone-paved drive, admiring the beautiful landscaping, when the house came in to view. It was one notch short of a colonial palace complete with double-curved staircases leading to the front door. It sat on the high ground with a commanding view of the town and the Atlantic.

Crafton opened the door immediately, "Hello, Patrick. Come right in, please. No trouble finding the place, I see."

"None at all. I got here a little early and drove around. Beautiful place. Tiny little shack, eh? My place could fit inside here five times, I think."

Crafton laughed. "Thanks. We decided to get a nice place when the kids were small. That way we could raise them in one spot and it would be home to them. We improved it a step at a time over the years. Janet, my wife, has a very good eye for design and color. She does it all. Care for the nickel tour?"

I nodded, but my stomach sank at the realization that I was one step backward now from ever affording a home like his.

"Just help me listen for the doorbell," he said. "The club is sending over a pizza and salads for us. Should be here in 10 minutes."

We walked around the first floor and looked at the rooms, which seemed to never end. He walked me into a massive theater room with lush carpet, gray leather seats much better than the movie theater, and a wide projector screen against one wall. Then we swung by the bar and grabbed a couple of beers and headed out to the back deck. It was spacious and had a commanding view of Marblehead Neck.

"Al, is it a deed restriction that you have to own a yacht to live here?" Boats were everywhere, big ones, sailing and power. Every point of the compass looked like a postcard.

"If you are going to live here, you might as well enjoy the water," Al summarized.

"Al, as I drove around, I saw that some estates have names on little signs. Does yours?"

"Not officially," he said. "But our family does have a special name for it. It's kind of our shorthand way of referencing the goal of leading the good life, which is life with balance."

"What do you call it?" I needed to know.

"The house on the hill," he said.

I sipped the Corona and shook my head. Beautiful.

"It's a nice home, sure, but the name symbolizes living well physically, intellectually, emotionally, financially, and especially spiritually. The house on the hill is the place where we live our highest dreams," Al explained.

He paused and let that thought sink in. What I had been doing seemed to put me ahead, but it had all come unraveled, and living my highest dreams seemed a long way off. Maybe it showed on my face.

"Long stressful day?" Al said.

"Yes."

He tipped his bottle toward mine, to toast. "To Plan B," he said, clinking the bottles.

"To Plan B," I said. "Whatever that is."

"Remember, there are no accidents. Plan B is often better than Plan A."

I looked around "Yup, I was right to set my sights on CEO. Now nobody will ever talk me out of it."

"And no one should. Maybe this event will propel you one step closer to your goal. If you stop to evaluate, learn, and grow, of course."

"I plan to. I plan to carefully consider my alternatives."

"Patrick, there's more to life than the corner office. You can have that and more. Next time you'll realize that, and you'll choose a better corporate culture. You'll be more balanced in your personal life too."

"Balance. Yes, I hope so. I wouldn't exactly say I've been very balanced in my life."

"You've focused only on your career," Crafton said. "But look where that gets us. Nowhere by itself. In the end, it's not what matters most. It's part of the picture and is a means to an end for some of the other components of a fulfilling life."

"I need some resources quick. I don't have much time before my financial tank is on empty."

"But you have savings, right?"

I shook my head. "Not really."

"But what about the basic principle of keeping three to six months of salary saved up in case of an emergency?"

"I guess I always thought that was for everyone else. I never really planned for an emergency."

"You need a financial advisor," Crafton said. "A coach who can help you with this. We can't be experts in all areas, Patrick. And if there's anything I've learned that's been a great help to me, it's to plan for the unanticipated to arise. I leave myself a financial margin, just in case, and also a personal time margin for any unexpected demands that pop up on short notice. Personal margin, a great concept."

"A time margin?"

"Yes. I don't cram my life to the brim with activities. I leave a margin of time for unexpected people or events that come into my world. If someone I love gets sick, for instance, it would be important to have time to dedicate to that person. You can't offer it if you don't have it to give. The future is uncertain, and it's hard to have peace and confidence in our daily lives if we are scheduled to the max and spending everything available."

"Al, I don't have the money to pay a financial planner to help me," I was embarrassed to say it.

"Trust me, Patrick, you need some breathing room, otherwise you will be stampeded into a bad career choice by financial pressure. If a planner is worth his or her fee, he or she will find the leeway in your situation for the fee and a whole lot of breathing room for you at this important juncture. I have a guy you can call, and I bet he will do a quick review and show you the possibilities before he flips on the meter," Al offered.

The doorbell rang and Crafton retreated to the front of the house. He returned with the pizza box and salads, placing them on the family dining table just off the kitchen. He motioned me in.

"Get a knife and some forks from the second drawer there."

He put two plates out on the table and handed me a heavy cloth napkin.

"So today was one to remember," I said. "It started with a lunch with Hannah. She got mad at me and left."

"Really?"

I nodded between bites. "Yeah, I told her about my stress at the office."

"And?"

"Basically she said I'd been a selfish, self-centered jerk, focused only on my career throughout our marriage. She said the only reason I was having lunch with her was because I was disillusioned about work...temporarily."

"Really? She said that?"

"Not in those words." Al and I laughed. I already felt lighter.

"Real change is not easy," Al said, "but it begins with deep desire. It involves getting in touch with our true values, what we stand for, the deep longings of our hearts."

"Is Dr. Phil about to show up? Because if he is, I need to get myself another beer." I stood, grabbed a beer from the counter, and opened it.

"Janet and I do not have the perfect marriage," Crafton said. "It's somewhat like a garden, and has to be tended all the time, fertilized, watered, and weeded. But on this I am clear, Patrick, that there is no success away from the family that will fully compensate for failure at home."

"I know that now," I said. "I don't want to climb the ladder of success and get to the top alone."

"Patrick, the way you prioritize will show Hannah what's most important in your life. I am not telling you how to prioritize and think. I am telling you to be intentional about it."

Crafton said nothing more, which invited me to say more than I intended.

"It became clear to me today that if I want to be married and have a family, and I do, I want it to be with Hannah. I know her and love her. Hell, we are already married. She is my wife. We are separated because of my behavior. I ignored her needs. If we divorce and I eventually marry someone else without fixing my problems, it will happen again . . . and maybe again, until I do the fix. If I've got to fix it anyway, why not do it now, and stay with Hannah."

"You figured all that out on your own?"

"With a little help from my friend."

"That is some good work, Patrick. You get an A+ in the practice of evaluating your experience. Nice piece of solo flying, young pilot! Now you just need a simple plan with clear first steps to begin to make those changes. The good news is that success feeds on itself."

I couldn't help laughing out loud. Al was perplexed. "You are like Mr. Miyagi in *The Karate Kid*. You know that movie?" I asked.

"Yes, I do. The student wanted to learn karate. The old teacher put him to work waxing the car and doing other work with very specific and demanding movements. Wax on, wax off; paint the fence. . . . It all came together in the end when the student combined the movements he had mastered and used them to achieve success in the ring."

"Al, I still don't know why you have taken me on as a student, but I am very grateful. I want a black belt."

"In time, Patrick. You have all the seeds of greatness. Don't let others sidetrack you from success by getting angry or emotional. You have a world-class opportunity here. What happens to us in life is less important than the way we respond to it. You have two choices. You were fired today. You can decide if it's an unfair calamity in your life based on lies, or you can decide if it is a wonderful gift. You and only you can make that determination, and your choice drives the outcome. A victim will determine it's a calamity and tell his or her life story from that reference point. Heroic people make the decision to evaluate, learn, and push forward to be better than ever."

"I plan to be the heroic one," I said.

"Good. Not easy, but worth it."

"I mean, I know I could go see a lawyer and serve Goodwin and Meyer with some sort of summons that would lock down the voice mail records and rub Patricia Redmond's nose in what Carter did, and ultimately expose the liar. Then I could use that to leverage whatever I could get. Might be rehired or get a cash settlement, Carter might be fired, and eventually everyone would know I was innocent and he was the villain. But I want to be bigger than that."

"What is at the other end of that spectrum?"

"Do nothing, get on with life and do well. I have decided to do nothing for seven days. Roll the video and think hard about my future. I'm not squeezing toothpaste for a week."

"Call me any time, Patrick," he said. "Whatever you need."

I smiled. "Another piece of pizza is good for now."

"You got it, my friend."

About 30 minutes later I was headed south on Cambridge Street with a piece of pizza wrapped in foil for breakfast and a date for Tuesday breakfast with Al at Fred's.

NINE

MARGE PLACED MY first mug of coffee on the table a little after 7 o'clock the following Tuesday.

"Hello, son. You're early, aren't you?" She put a well-worn plastic glass of water with hints of chlorine beside the coffee.

"Right, a little. Al's due at 8:00. Big day. I couldn't wait."

"We do have a great friend, don't we?" she offered a rare smile.

"Marge, when did you first meet Al?" I asked. "Did you meet him here?"

She shook her head. "Nope, over at HOPE Center when I showed up there 11 years ago at the end of my rope. Al was my primary coach for almost 2 years. He saved me, and more than that, he saved my boy. My husband was abusive, and I was living on the street with my 10-year-old."

"Really? I'm sorry."

"No need to be. HOPE Center and Al Crafton helped turn my life around. They gave me opportunity, and dignity. Scott was able to go to school."

"Where is your son now?"

"He's graduating from college soon, if you can believe that. Went to the University of Maine, and he's getting his degree in forestry, with honors," she curtseyed.

"You must be very proud."

"You bet! And I'm forever grateful to Al. He really gives the best possible tips!" She laughed out loud at her own joke.

"What is Al helping you with?" she asked.

I summarized the last 10 weeks for her in about four sentences, emphasizing my determination to use this reboot of my life for greater progress. I explained how we had met by accident on the plane.

"There are no accidents," she said, and we both smiled.

"You're right, Marge. There are no accidents."

"Times like you are going through are defining moments, Al would say." She stepped closer and gripped my shoulder as Al walked up.

"You two up to some funny business?" he asked.

Marge rolled her eyes. She poured his coffee and went to place our order with the kitchen.

I pointed to my watch.

"Yeah yeah, I know, you beat me again. Why'd you get here so early?" He settled in, looked around. A man from across the restaurant came over and thanked him for helping him out with a flat tire the week before. "I made it to my appointment because of you," the man said, grinning. "By the skin of my teeth."

I looked at Al and shook my head. "You know how to fix a flat? Is there anything you don't know how to do?"

"Not really," he said, with a confident head move and a big grin.

"Oh brother."

The man slid into the booth beside me. "My name's Bill," he said, shaking my hand. He wore jeans and a white work shirt with a soda company logo. There was a large truck parked outside with the same markings.

"You a driver?"

"I am," he said. "Been doing it for 20 years. Known Al almost as long." He looked over at the three-by-five card in front of me. "What's this all about? Are you in school with Al?" His fingers gripped the edge of the card. They were thick and calloused.

"I am," I said. "Want to hear what I've been thinking?" I looked at Al, and he smiled.

"While I've had some ups and downs this week, I've really tried to use this time for planning. I've been thinking a lot about the future. First item on the card is home life. I want a good home life. I want a wife and, no, wait . . . scratch that. I don't want just any wife, I want mine. I want Hannah back. Then together if we decide to have kids, that's a second goal." I pointed to the card. "See?"

Bill turned it around in his hand so that Al could see it. "He's right. It's right there! In black and white!"

"Note that number 3 on the list is career. I want to be a good provider by having a very successful career. I want career success for my family and myself. I'm wired that way. Also, you talk about balance a lot. I want it. Will you tell me more about what it is and how to get it?"

I looked at Bill. "I need to get you updated on the notes on the card. My wife threw me out. I got fired. I have my back against the wall financially, and here I am dreaming about balance not really knowing what it is. Got it?"

The man shook his head. He lifted an arm in the air. "Margie, can I have some coffee?" he said loudly. He turned back. "Boy, I'm going to need some fuel to understand all of this mess."

Marge delivered our plates and poured Bill his coffee. "You want the same thing you always get, you old coot?"

"You gonna talk to me that way in front of friends?" he said, playing back.

I began peppering my food. Al took a bite of eggs and looked over.

"Patrick, would you help Castle with some interim work we need?" He pushed a business card across the table. "This is Ross Dolins, one of my EVPs leading a project of great importance to us. It is a possible acquisition, and the team could use some more horsepower and current insight at this stage. Call Ross to discuss it, but we have in mind a six- to eight-week engagement as a consultant for you to help us out."

I was dumbfounded. "A consultant?"

"Your recent experience will be a great asset, Patrick."

I looked away. I didn't know what else to say.

"He's right!" Bill said.

"Let's see then," Al continued. "You spoke of balance. We all want to be happy, but you don't have to settle for just that. It's like the corner office; you can have that on the way to life's deeper riches, but you need to define what they are. That's work only you can do."

"You think being happy is settling for less?"

"I know that may sound different, but let me ask you a question. Would you rather be happy, or would you rather live a life of significance, deep joy, real connection to other people, and know your purpose and fulfill it? It's a lot more than mere happiness."

"No comparison."

"You and I agree. That's why I say there is real sustaining and drawing power in getting clear on what you will stand for, your deepest personal values. And they may evolve slowly. That's okay."

"Al, when we first met, you asked me what I wanted to do with it if I made a lot of money, remember?"

"Of course, and you blew off that question."

"I did, sorry. But this is what you were talking about, right?"

"Right. You are connecting the dots. For me, significance mostly has to do with serving other people. We all love being served, but ultimately I have come to understand that the servant is the one fulfilled. It's like helping Bill fix the flat the other day. It was my honor."

"Not everyone sees things that way," I said, "No offense, Bill, but I think if you had asked me to fix the flat, you would have missed the meeting."

Bill threw his head back and laughed.

"So tell me more about Hannah," Al said.

"I saw Hannah twice over the weekend. We met Saturday afternoon and had a glass of wine. I was able to tell her that her concern that she had expressed at the sushi place had really struck me, that I had chased after her, but then thought better of it because I wanted to think about whether she was right."

"Is that all?"

"No. I'm happy to say that she must have been convinced I was sincere. We spent Sunday afternoon together. I picked her up, and we went for a walk in the park and talked. There was no agenda; it was just the two of us. I found that I really enjoyed asking her questions and listening carefully to her answers. She's a special girl."

"And Superman?"

I stared at him. It didn't register.

"The guy she was seeing. What about him?"

"She called him and broke it off. She said she told him she isn't in as big a hurry as he is and it isn't fair to him. Al, I think I have a shot at getting this thing healed."

"That's big news," Al said.

"My plan is to just spend time with her for now. Hopefully show her my new thinking. If it is meant to be, it will be. I don't have to drive it."

"Marriage is like formation flying," Al said. "Independent pilots, choosing to fly very close together, in a two-ship unit for mutual benefit. Each with certain roles and responsibilities for the common objective. Formations give multiplied power, but both members have to pay attention all the time. When they do, it is almost magic."

"See, I'm listening and learning. But we need to get going. You are due around the corner, I bet."

"Yes, and you have a phone call to make."

We all stood. "Bill, great to meet you," I said.

"You too, Patrick."

Al paid the check, left a great tip, and suggested that we lunch at the Harbor Club for our next session on a date to be selected after I knew my consulting schedule. I wondered if the Harbor Club lunch was where he held final sessions with his "arrows." That thought made my heart race with a little panic.

TEN

THE WELCOME LOBBY of the Harbor Club was more impressive than I remembered. A man and a woman were standing 20 feet apart talking on their cell phones. The man was Al Crafton, and when he spotted me, he waved, then held up two fingers.

True to his prediction, it was two minutes later when Al tucked away his phone extended his hand and said, "Patrick! Glad this worked out."

"Me too, Al. Only my second time here."

"Let's go in. They are holding a table by the window for us. What time is your next appointment?"

"I have a meeting at 2:30, but I'm already prepped for it."

We were escorted to a table with a perfect view of the sparkling harbor. The hostess removed the white napkins from the table and quickly substituted black ones.

"What's this for?" I asked.

"Keeps the lint off of your suit, Patrick."

I nodded, and felt dumb for asking.

"So tell me how you think the consulting assignment is going with Ross and the team."

I sat up a little straighter. "The acquisition is a big one. If we get the right structure and services transition agreement to keep their key management and goodwill in place, I think 40 percent in two years is conservative."

"Interesting," Al touched his chin.

"But we have some important due diligence yet to go. We've identified two areas that need careful analysis. Either one could be a deal killer. It's where I've seen inflated pro formas before. If someone wants to hide a ball on us, it could be there. But if those numbers prove solid, they are probably trustworthy people across the board."

"Ross filled me in. He said this was all you, Patrick, and was spot on. His team was not focused there. You have helped already in a huge way. Give me your gut feel."

"You know your street nickname, don't you? Al Craftsman, outta respect for your skill. And you want me to guess?"

"No, not guess. Gut feel. There's a difference."

"Okay, my gut says that this deal may be too good to be true. I've asked Ross to put me as close as possible to all communication with your two banking firms. We may be able to get some sense as to who else is being courted. That could tell us something. But mainly we need to go deep on these two actuarial analyses. I know of a small actuarial consulting firm that is really ahead of the rest on sensitivity testing. I think Ross is going to use them."

"What's going on with Goodwin and Meyer?"

"Nothing at all. I'm not going to make an issue about the voice mails and Carter's role in it. I've moved on. The consulting engagement is perfect for me right now. Thanks again."

"Hannah?"

"More of the same, all good. We are spending time together and really talking. I loved her before, but I'm learning that there is so much more there. She seems guarded, but she's giving me an opportunity. That's all I can ask."

"Well said. I want to meet her one day."

"She feels the same way. Let's make it happen. Which brings up something I have been wondering about."

"What would that be?"

"Is this our last meeting?"

"Oh, you have had enough, have you? Calling a halt?"

"I think you know better. I need more, but I just wonder how much time you are willing to invest," I admitted, recognizing my fear.

"Let's come back to that, but for now, let's make the most use of this meeting. Fair enough?"

"Sure, you want to talk about balance now?" I offered.

He smiled. "In fact, I do. Each of those five areas of your life that we talked about is important. Patrick, the difference between first and second place is often a quarter of an inch. I find consistent, sustained behavior, driven by a strong and balanced base offers you an edge."

"Al, you say each of these five categories have common characteristics and are driven by simple principles. Thanks to you I know that it's not just about work. It's not about making money or climbing the corporate ladder. It's about total life prosperity and being healthy in all categories."

"That's right," he said. "For instance, physical health. You want to maintain it for two reasons. What are they?"

"Well, longevity obviously. That's one. And feeling good and healthy is another. That close?"

"You got it. The components of good health are weight, exercise, and monitoring. Weight is the simple result of intake versus output."

"Sounds simple," I said.

"It is. That's the power, simplicity. Get that framework in your head, and it helps you do better at the dozens of little choices you have to make every day that determine your health," Al said.

"Okay, got it."

"Simple analysis helps us understand the drivers in all areas of life. In the financial area, the first requirement is to learn to live well not on what you make but consistently on less than you make. You must furnish your own funds. Fail at this and nothing else matters; you will not succeed in this area of life. And again, it is the function of income versus outgo. It is faster and more efficient to address outgo to get better results in the financial area. You can control your spending right now. Improving income takes longer."

"I can see that, especially when I'm honest with myself about how I've handled, actually mishandled, my own money despite my good salary."

"Overspending, which is spending what you make or more, is a big problem for Americans at all levels, individual family, corporate, and government levels. Overspending leads to debt. The goal is no debt. Debt simply increases your cost of goods and services and keeps you enslaved. A good exercise to motivate yourself is to list your debts, both principal and rate of interest. Then multiply to get the annual interest you are paying at the current cross section of balances and interest rates.

For instance, if you have a credit card with a $15,000 balance and you are paying 15 percent interest, that's $2,250 in annual interest. Total up all those numbers for all of your debt and divide by 12 to figure out the monthly rent you are paying to use other people's money. Don't be surprised if it's several hundred dollars monthly. Then put that monthly amount on a compound interest chart and see what power that level of savings and investment has at an equity return rate of a modest 12 percent annually until you are age 55 or 60. It'll be a big number. A very big number.

The question is, whom do you want your money to work for, 'them' or you? I am dismayed at how otherwise smart people of all ages open a financial vein and sit watching it bleed, all the time frustrated that they are not getting ahead. Passenger mentality at its worst." Al shook his head suddenly. "Sorry for the soapbox."

"No, don't apologize." I mock slapped my cheek. "I needed that. I work in the financial field every day, but I have royally messed up my own affairs."

"Patrick, you are not alone. Most people are the same way. Also, when you find yourself back in your marriage, money should be a team sport. It will be an issue in your household. You decide whether it is a point of strength and agreement or a point of stress," Al said.

"I can see that. Anything else on money?"

"Last item, once you control spending and get debts reduced so you're beginning to actually save, you can get a professional financial planner involved. You would not be your own lawyer or doctor. Don't settle for your own amateur expertise in this complex area either."

"You're right."

"Of course I am," he said smiling.

"I hope to someday help others the way you do, Al."

"You'll find it very gratifying, but I encourage you not to wait until you have all the answers. If you do, you'll never begin. It's not all about you, Patrick, and it's not about me. Reaching out to others leaves the best legacy."

I nodded. I knew he was right.

"Invariably I find when I am getting off balance in my mind, viewpoint, or heart, I have become overfocused on myself. Refocusing on other people and the many positive things in my life gets me back on track. There's a lot of poor counsel that floats around promising easy fixes and simple keys to greatness. Patrick, we all have the chance to know ourselves well, but we view our own strengths and weaknesses through distorted lenses. We just have to lay all that down and be brutally honest in our ongoing self-assessment. Then, when we have identified something we really wish was better, we dig, gently work on it, and grow in that area."

The waiter came, cleared our plates, refilled our water, and offered dessert. Al ordered coffee, and I asked for sparkling water with lime.

"Any model for analyzing a complex subject will have its defects. Dividing life into five parts implies that the parts are more separate and distinct than is actually true.

Intellect resides in the brain. So the brain's physical health must be maintained."

"I can see that. Assuming you get blood and oxygen to your brain, what else can you do for your intellect?"

"Again, use it or lose it. Do you read much?"

"Not enough."

"I became a reader only in recent years, but now I usually have a fiction and a nonfiction going at all times. I also try to engage in mind-stretching conversations with significant people. I like to discuss bigger issues."

"Bet you don't watch much TV," I offered.

"Sometimes. But you're right, not much. I like to filter what comes in, and what goes out."

I smiled. "Like an athlete, huh?"

"What we put into our minds is just as important as what we put into our bodies," he said. "And, yes, it is a bit like being an athlete. If you're aiming for peak performance in all areas of your life, you're intentional about what you listen to, whom you spend time with, and especially where you train your thinking time."

"Can I ask you a question?"

"Sure," he said. "Anything."

"You've taught me so much during our time together. But what have you gotten out of it?"

Crafton thought for a moment. "Patrick, this time with you has been just as valuable for me. To be honest with you, I've learned that there's still a lot more I can do in this life."

I laughed. "How so? You've already done it all. You lead a major company, you give back to the community, you help people . . ."

"But there are always more ways to grow, Patrick. I've seen how much you've grown, and it's inspired me. I think I kind of hit a plateau in my own life, and now it's time for me to set new goals, with higher expectations. Just because you've had some success doesn't mean there isn't something else to learn. We're always learning and growing. God always has more for us and has given us great capacity. He wants us to use it well."

I looked at him. I wasn't sure what to think about that last one.

"Do you believe that in your own life?" he asked.

"I don't know. I have a lot of doubts and misgivings, let's just say that."

"Most people sense that this life is not all there is," Crafton said. "Wouldn't you agree?"

"Sure."

"All I'm saying is that your life isn't an accident. There's a plan for your life, and you have a legacy to live out during your time on this planet."

"Hard to argue with that."

"Yes, it is, but I did just that when I was your age. I argued and resisted until I was 40 years old. But then I realized that my life was a lot bigger than I thought. There had been a master plan all along. It was a relief to learn I did not have to do it all myself, alone. I was not limited by my own best thinking, so to speak. Patrick, all the peaks and valleys, the trials and tribulations, it's all for a reason. In the end, you're going to have had real and lasting impact on the world. We can talk about that more when you are ready." Al smiled and checked his watch. "Next Tuesday, Fred's, 7:30?"

"Sounds great," I said.

"Before we go, I have a little gift for you. I noticed you like French cuffs."

Al slid a black velvet box across the table. "You've earned these," he said.

I took the box and opened it slowly. Inside were two simple cufflinks. Silver pilot wings, perfect miniature size.

I was immediately overwhelmed by his gesture. I choked back tears. I looked out across Boston Harbor and thought about the things he had said about my life, and my destiny. I glanced back at Al and he looked away as he brushed his cheek with his black napkin.

ACKNOWLEDGMENTS

Lamar Smith

Dr. David J. Schwartz was chairman of the Marketing Department at my college and the author of *The Magic of Thinking Big*. For his book, his teaching in class, and his catalytic enthusiasm, I will be forever grateful. Dr. Schwartz's insight and gifts live on in his writings, and his example is one I have kept in mind for many years. His work has caused so many people to begin thinking differently, with me among them.

Early in my business career I ran into the work of Zig Ziglar. Attitude, intent to serve, and communications techniques truly are critical. You made it understandable.

For seven years I had the privilege of serving George Talley, a former admiral in the U.S. Navy and CEO of our financial planning firm, as his president. George taught much, and every now and then he would use words. For his lighthearted wisdom, I am thankful.

ACKNOWLEDGMENTS

John Ott, Preston Gillham, and the rest of the SWAT team are men of wisdom and heart. They live lives that matter and help others do the same.

Bill Kraftson is one of the best friends anyone can have. For being allowed to know his tough tenderness, his deep knowledge offered with a deft touch, his commitment to real significance, and so much more, I am in debt.

Writing a book is misery and fun. Several helped alleviate the misery and emphasize the fun. Tammy Kling, the mistress of the pen, was chief among them. "Show don't tell, less is more, allow the reader some room, and have fun with this" were key messages she taught. I hope I can learn them one day.

Help with the concept and the manuscript was offered by several friends and principally include Preston Gillham, Kevin Dunn, and Janet Kraftson. You made it better.

Knox Huston, our editor, and his team at McGraw-Hill could not have been more effective or professional while making the journey enjoyable. Knox, you are thoughtful, wise, and gentle—a great combination.

Finally, a special thanks to the ladies in my life, wife, Jan, and daughter, Meg. Jan, you set the standard. I am eternally grateful for your love and encouragement. And Meg, your input has been special. Your keen mind and personal values coupled with your love for books and people refresh and inspire.

ACKNOWLEDGMENTS

TAMMY KLING

Writing a book is often a great battle of the soul. You explore all aspects of yourself to find the right meaning, and then you do it all over again when it's not quite right. In all of it, you think about the reader. I'd like to acknowledge you, the reader. As we pondered you, and the title that reflected the office, it's worthy to note now that we were always thinking about the value and nobility of every profession, whether it be a consultant, an artist, a bus driver, or an executive striving for the corner office. I'd like to acknowledge all of those on the journey, because this book is more about the story of our individual journey itself than the office, cubicle, or corporate organization we may choose. I'd also like to acknowledge the One who made the inspiration possible, and my gifts in life, namely, Reed, Luke, and Mark, who support my creating at all hours of the day and night. Thanks once more to our fabulous and brilliant team at McGraw-Hill and especially to KH, who believed in the message of this book.

ABOUT THE AUTHORS

LAMAR SMITH was highly decorated as a U.S. Air Force pilot for directing combat search-and-rescue missions and other Special Forces work during the Viet Nam war. After his military career he entered the financial planning industry as an advisor, and after seven years he became president of his firm. Subsequently he was named CEO. He continued in that role for 15 years, during a period of progress and growth, servicing more than 300,000 client families and overseeing $18 billion of investment assets, $52 billion of life insurance, and a successful bank. Lamar left the corporate officer world in 2007 and now actively serves on a variety of corporate and nonprofit organization boards.

TAMMY KLING is an international author whose books have been sold in countries across the globe and have been featured in the *New York Times* and *Wall Street Journal*. She has written books with major organizations and CEOs, including the Dial Corporation and Wrigley. She has a background in crisis management as an airline crash team manager, and wrote her second book, *Exit Row*, about that experience. Tammy has appeared on *Dateline NBC*, *Geraldo*, and several other national shows promoting her books. She writes with the hope of transforming lives through the written word.

For more information about

the authors

Lamar Smith and Tammy Kling,

the **benefits** of **balanced living**, and

how to **achieve balance** in your **life**…

go to:

www.ImprovingYourBalance.com